Damage Control

Heart Breaks to Heart Saves!

One mother's personal story of turning tragedy to triumph!

SHARON BATES

ISBN Hardcover: 978-1-64184-436-9
ISBN Paperback: 978-1-64184-437-6
ISBN eBook: 978-1-64184-438-3

Preface

Sharon Bates is a caring, determined woman. She has devoted her life to developing and implementing her program to save lives throughout the country. After losing her son, Anthony Bates, to an undetected heart condition, prompted her to promote nationwide heart testing in school systems and athletic programs to detect such heart conditions. Thus, she has been responsible for saving thousands of lives.

Sharon's non-profit work became her lifetime commitment through her amazing love for her son and her devotion to saving lives. Her path has not been an easy one, but her persistence has carried her through it.

With great respect and love,

Bill Snyder
Head Football Coach
Kansas State University (1989-2005, 2009-2018)
Anthony's Coach (1999 – 2000)

Dedication

I dedicate this book to my son, Anthony. With his drive and dedication to football, he showed me how to become a better person. Additionally, I dedicate these words of wisdom to all parents that walk the "grief journey." You will find your way and light the path of love with the love you have shared with your child.

My grateful heart is forever indebted to my love, Will Maier. He encouraged me to write the story of my life and love for my son. He also came up with the title. He picked it because it epitomized his definition of the term. Accordingly, "Damage Control is a mindset about recovering from an indescribable loss through attitude, skills, and perseverance: to 'keep going' under all circumstances, effectively dealing with whatever challenges you encounter." Will also did significant editing on my manuscript. Thank you, Will!

Table of Contents

Author's Note

Grief Journey

How can I move forward in this bizarre-world? I started on my "grief journey" on July 31, 2000, after my son and only child, Anthony Bates, died from an undiagnosed heart condition. The pain and anguish from such a significant loss are beyond words. My sorrow's depth is more profound than the Grand Canyon, broader and deeper than all the oceans. Through this experience, I needed to continue my life to prove that I could persevere, make my way through the sadness, overcome the anger, and search for happiness. I am not a grief expert, only on my pain. I write these words and accounts of the happenings in my life to show that we must overcome these challenges, no matter the temporary events. I had to honor my son, honor my life, and show that **I am still standing.**

My heart aches every time another child dies from Sudden Cardiac Arrest (SCA) in this country. According to the Institute of Medicine (IOM) study from 2015[1] They estimate that over 12,000 youth suffer

---

[1]   Strategies to Improve Cardiac Arrest Survival: A Time to Act, Robert Graham, Margaret A. McCoy, and Andrea M. Schultz, Institute of Medicine of the National Academies, ISBN 978-0-309-37199-5 | DOI 10.17226/21723, June 2015

SCA every year. American Heart Association (AHA) claims there are over 300,000 victims of SCA every year. Regrettably, only eight percent of these victims survive out-of-hospital SCA. The numbers are staggering and somewhat disheartening. There is light at the end of the tunnel of this grieving process called a "grief journey." Some grassroots organizations are making headway on the reduction of Sudden Cardiac Death (SCD) in the U.S. It takes a village to save a life, and this book is full of the stories of the villagers that came to my rescue.

Call to Action – Kids are Dying.
What are we going to do?

What can we do to prevent these tragedies?

Is the problem too big to make a difference in our lifetime? Shouldn't our schools and sports programs inform parents and the student-athletes about the risks of Sudden Cardiac Arrest (SCA)?

Before entering college, perhaps as early as middle school, parents and student-athletes should be availed of heart disease information in youth. The risk of not knowing your child's heart health before playing a sport is dangerous. Schools and sports programs allow and share more support to the programs providing heart-screening tests to youth and their families. The programs offered will save young lives and prevent much of the Sudden Cardiac Death on the playing field. *This issue truly is a matter of life and death.*

Sports are not just about winning or losing, but must also be about your child's health and life! Make an informed decision of the risks of the sport of choice. There have been studies going back to the early 1960s, stating the risk of cardiac maladies with young athletes. *Why* do we continue to ignore the facts? We don't need any more "long-term studies" or "wasted research funds" when previous studies have concluded that children's lives are at risk of Sudden Cardiac Death. A child's life is precious, and without heart tests, a child's life is at risk of Sudden Cardiac Death.

Parents can take control of their child's health. In your communities, seek out heart-screening programs already in place. Over 1,000 organizations, hospitals, and community partners offer free and low-cost heart-screenings. Find the ones in your community and your state. Support the cause and bring your children in for heart tests.

If you don't have those programs in your community, demand heart tests at your child's sports physicals. The more parents, sports leagues, and people who speak up and make the demands of their health-care providers and insurance providers, the more likely the providers will make changes for the benefit of your family. Keep in mind that a health-care provider will only provide the care for which the insurance companies will pay. Insurance companies are "for-profit" and consider extra tests incidental and unnecessary. Your child's life is precious and matters to you and your family. Be your child's health advocate.

You can be proactive and start something for your community. Create a heart-screening program! Don't wait for a child to die to take action. All children's lives are valuable, and each deserves a chance of a full, productive life.

The sports industry needs to make all sports safer. That must be the cornerstone of any game. Find the flaw, correct, and improve. This book is the challenge to address safety in sporting events for children. If you are reading this book and are in the sporting field, I encourage you to make a difference in your sport.

As for the NCAA, you must protect your athletes in college. The case of disgraced, now incarcerated, Dr. Larry Nassar is an excellent example of a horrible nightmare for young women in women's gymnastics. There were too many people looking the other way, not taking a stand for their athletes. If you are reading this book and connected with NCAA sports, I encourage you to make a difference in your college and the competition you represent.

National sports authorities aim to protect more than 8 million high school and junior high school athletes. Those numbers are staggering, but so are the "at-risk" statistics shown with the mass screening groups. Over 160,000 youth are at risk of Sudden Cardiac Death. The Anthony Bates Foundation (ABF) Trained Teams started screening hearts in 2001. Through 2020, ABF Trained Teams have provided more than 1,013,745 young athlete screenings. Our statistics show well over 20,000 could have findings that are "Possible Life-Threatening"(two percent.) On the other hand, possibly more than 20,000 were at risk of Sudden Cardiac Death, and their lives saved through our screenings.

Each school district is responsible for the safety and well-being of its student-athletes. The school districts need to inform the parents and student-athletes about the risk of a Sudden Cardiac Death (SCD). Additionally, every school that hosts high school and junior high school sports must have Automatic External Defibrillators (AEDs) and an Emergency Preparedness Plan (EPP) to protect the students and visitors of SCD. If a child dies during a school day or school event without these life-saving measures, the school district risks $2.5 million or more in a lawsuit. AEDs and EPPs are the standards of care. ***You MUST be prepared to protect ALL the lives in your school.*** The school is responsible not only for the students at risk but also for the staff and visitors who are at risk of sudden cardiac arrest.

Be prepared for the "emergency" before you become "emergency."

Schools can and should be the location of heart-screening events for young athletes in their care. Prevention is our key to a lifetime of health.

I don't have all the answers, but I do have the "heart," experience, and empirical data to have made a difference in over a million young lives!

My life became empty, and my heart shattered when my only child, Anthony, died. To build a national youth heart-health movement, I have worked tirelessly with little pay, over the last twenty years.

No parent should experience and struggle with the level of grief that nearly destroyed my soul.

I have endured years of alone time, years of working, and ferreting out the truth of the issues at hand. It's time for me to shout out the TRUTH about what needs to happen and keep our children safe from Sudden Cardiac Arrest!

My heart hurts to think I would let my son down if I walked away from screening or supporting our cause. Although, I know he honestly would understand. Yet, I am filled with joy to see new faces stepping into the picture to help us "screen young hearts and save young lives!" We will do more together. You are part of the "we" in my village! The connection of "our village" encourages us to ban together, continuing to take ABF to new heights, as we enter our third decade of active service.

CHAPTER ONE

July 31, 2000

The sun was hot in Manhattan, Kansas, a.k.a. "The Little Apple," and the air stale with the smell of cattle. Anthony had just completed the last summer workout before the Kansas State University football season activities began. He picked up his green gym bag with his workout gloves and weightlifting belt and yelled after the weight room staff and guys still lifting, "I'm going to make like a tree and get out of here!" which was his funny way of misusing a reference through a movie quote. Then he was gone.

His red truck was in the football complex parking lot. He got in to head home for lunch. But, he didn't make it back home that day. When Anthony rounded the corner on Anderson and Dennison streets in Manhattan, he went into Sudden Cardiac Arrest (SCA). The episode didn't subside. He passed out while driving and struck an oncoming vehicle then crashed into a parked car just blocks from the Manhattan fire department.

Even before the crash, emergency calls immediately came into the 911 operator, as witnesses saw him driving erratically seemingly slumped against the driver's side window. Fire and Rescue were on the scene within a minute of the impact. Anthony was in distress, they got him out of his truck, and the ambulance arrived to take him to Mercy Hospital, which was only a mile from the scene.

About forty-five minutes into Anthony's emergency, I received what seemed to be a routine phone call on my cell phone at work, "Sharon, this is Coach Latimore!"

"Coach, thanks for calling me back." I had called him the Friday before as Anthony had complained he was not doing well with his summer workouts. He thought he had gained too much weight over the summer. It turned out that Anthony was in heart failure, and the excessive water weight he was carrying was due to the inefficiencies of his heart.

"No, Sharon, I'm calling you because Anthony has been in a car accident!" Coach Latimore nervously explained.

"What!" I cried. My heart dropped in my chest — it was the worst call any mother could receive, especially with hundreds of miles separating me from my child. At that time, I was working and living in Little Ferry, New Jersey. Uncontrollable thoughts were whirling in my mind in a matter of seconds. "Is this serious? Do I need to get on a plane? Will he be okay?"

"The doctors asked if Anthony or your family have any heart issues," Coach Latimore inquired.

I blurted out, "No, not that I'm aware. Cancer, but no heart issues. Oh, wait, his biological father has a daughter that was born with a problem. But I don't know any details. Let me call you back."

My ex-husband, Joe, revealed that his youngest daughter, Dani, was born with a hole in her heart. This condition is somewhat common in children, but there were no other heart issues in his family or mine.

I replied on my return call, "Coach, Anthony has a half-sister with a hole in her heart at birth. Nothing else."

"Sharon, we need you to come to Manhattan now! It doesn't look good," Coach Latimore sadly reported.

Through my tears, I explained to my manager that I would be traveling to Kansas to be with my son. I left work and made a flurry of phone calls to family and friends. I made my way to my home and prepared for my trip to Kansas. The next phone call I got was from the hospital staff: **"Sharon, your son, didn't make it!"**

My world stopped. I sank to my knees, and I could not stop crying through the agony I was feeling. Uncontrollable tears flooded my eyes, and my body convulsed in gut-wrenching pain. The life that I once knew no longer existed. At that very moment, my life froze in time. My gut twisted in knots. Everything up to that point I did during the "emergency" was a reaction to the crisis. I was on "auto-pilot." When Anthony got hurt on the playground, I took care of his injuries and made it "all better." However, I had no answer to this tragedy. In just an instant, my son was dead. I didn't know how to act or react. I didn't know what to do next. I didn't know whom to call first with the bad news. I didn't know how I was supposed to feel. It seemed like I was having a nightmare with no end. I couldn't wake from this odd feeling. I was in total shock.

I quickly added a black dress to my packed suitcase, and I rushed to catch the next plane from Newark to Kansas City. I said good-bye to Maureen and Pete Iurato, the parents of Steve, my new fiancé. They had rushed up from Cape May when they heard the news about Anthony's emergency. Steve and I went to the airport, not knowing when we would return.

CHAPTER TWO

August 1, 2000

The wait for the plane from Newark to Kansas City was horrible. There were weather delays due to the summer storms across the country. We sat on the tarmac for an extra hour before we could take off. My uncontrollable sobbing punctured the silence. No words can describe the first moments and hours after losing my only child. I was such a mess on the plane ride; people kept their distance, not knowing what to say or console me in my first moments of deep sadness. My fiancé, Steve Iurato, accompanied me from New Jersey, and traveling from Phoenix, Arizona, was Allen Bates, Anthony's adopted-father, his real father figure, and my best friend, Roxane Watson.

Once in Kansas City, we made our way to the terminal for the small plane to Manhattan. We met up with Allen and Roxane in the Kansas City terminal. Aboard the short flight, I was numb to the world, Allen asked about Anthony's arrangements, saying, "I don't know what he wanted."

Over the airplane roar, I stated, "I do; he told me last Christmas." After the shooting murder of Derrick Wheaton, Phoenix College football teammate in Arizona, we talked about death and dying. We also discussed the sudden death of Nancy Bennett in Kansas, who was struck by lightning while jogging. Discussing death made our conversations so grim. Another sad occurrence in California was the death last December of a young high-school football player, Scotty Lang. Scotty's death was one of the topics Anthony and I shared on a phone call. With the New Year approaching and with Y2K doomsday reports, Anthony and I had talked about our possible funeral arrangements for each other upon our deaths. He told me he "wanted to be cremated and sprinkled at Winfield Lake," where Allen and I had taken him camping and fishing when we had lived in Wichita. The realization of our recent post-death conversations was very surreal!

He also shared with me he hoped I didn't have to take care of his arrangements. Of course, I was confused and asked him why. He said, "No parent should have to bury their child." That is when I thought he must have had some foresight into his future. "Sad, really sad and strange at the same time," I admitted to the group.

CHAPTER THREE

Anthony's Funeral

Some of the other coaches were close to Anthony, Head Defensive Coordinator, Coach Phil Bennett, and Defensive Line Coach Mo Latimore. These two coaches had the most direct interaction with Anthony.

Coach Bennett lost his wife precisely one year to the day of Anthony's funeral. It broke my heart to see him so crushed by her loss, and then twelve months after that to experience Anthony's loss. He was a good man and supported Anthony in his college football career.

The first summer that Anthony was at Kansas State University, there was an issue about my son staying on the football team. The D-line coach, Mo Latimore, was trying to get Anthony scrubbed from the team. Anthony knew he wasn't as talented as the other players on the line, but was doing his best to keep up and make a place for himself on the team.

Coach Latimore told Anthony he could be cut from the Kansas State University Football team for lack of performance. I contacted Coach Bennett and advocated for my son. Anthony was smart and talented. It was the responsibility of the coaches to work with him every day and help to make improvements. At least that was what I understood to have been stipulated in the twenty-five-page document that they signed together. It is interesting to me how easily an athlete is expendable to a college athletic program. In the end, Anthony was not cut from the team and was able to stay at Kansas State University until his death.

When Anthony died, one of the first phone calls I made was to my big sister, Brenda. She and her husband, Mark, drove from their home in Montana to Kansas to be with me before the funeral's dreaded day.

They made it to Manhattan, Kansas, in record time. They drove straight through, and I am grateful for their help, as I was in such a dense fog those first days and weeks. My sadness was so incredibly deep during the first moments of my trip to Kansas. With a flurry of activities, we made funeral arrangements. We set up some gatherings the day before and after the funeral, and we started to clean out his apartment, which all blended into a humongous heap of sadness.

Brenda and Mark were always by my side. We cried together and laughed about some of our memories of Anthony. Then we would cry without getting past the memory of our times together. My son was their nephew. He was a small child when they got married. They didn't have children right away, as Anthony would remind them of challenges of raising children, so they waited several years to start their own family. Brenda and Mark settled in Great Falls, Montana, as Mark's U.S. Air Force career took off.

When Anthony was in high school, Mark's Mom and Dad, Viv and Jim Laramore, still lived in Arizona. Brenda and Mark brought their family to Phoenix a few times for visits until they eventually moved his aging parents to Montana. Clinton (Clint) was the oldest child of the three Laramore children; then Melanie (Lanie), their middle child; and Gabrielle, the youngest. The Laramore clan would make another trip in 1997 to see Anthony play football for Phoenix College, against Ricks College in Boise, Idaho. I flew in, and Brenda drove from Montana. They had a little car trouble on that trip and swapped out the broken vehicle for a rental car to pick me up at the airport in Boise. We were so excited to see each other. I am happy we have that shared memory.

Mark spoke for our family at Anthony's funeral. I was such an emotional wreck; there was no way I could talk to the crowd. Mark was a Master Sergeant in the Air Force. Dressed in his blues, he made me so proud to represent our family. I am forever grateful to my brother (not technically, but Mark rates full "brotherhood" for stepping up to that difficult task!) Tons of love to my Laramore clan, and I will forever be grateful to you all.

When I started the Anthony Bates Foundation (ABF), I asked my sister, Brenda, to be on the Board of Advisors. She was gracious to accept and still serves on the board today. The Laramore family has been passionately supportive of ABF and all our vital work to prevent sudden cardiac arrest and death.

CHAPTER FOUR

What is Hypertrophic Cardiomyopathy (HCM)?

O ur family all stayed together in a local Manhattan hotel for the week before Anthony's funeral. My other two sisters, two of my nephews, and my mother flew in to be with us. Many of Allen's family members drove in from different parts of Kansas and Oklahoma. We all tried to wrap our minds around the senseless passing of a seemingly healthy young man in his life's prime. There we arranged for Anthony's funeral, visits to the football staff and many of the players, and time spent with arriving family. The overwhelming, excruciating pain of such a significant loss continued to make no sense and had no meaning.

The Shawnee County Coroner performed Anthony's autopsy. There was no coroner in Riley County, where he died. His body went to Topeka before most of the family, or I arrived in Manhattan. Anthony's Aunt Terry, Allen's older sister, lived in nearby Topeka and was able to view his body in the hospital before they sent it to the coroner. She later shared with the family that the experience was extremely uncomfortable, and she would not offer more details to spare the family additional heartache. I am grateful that she saved me from the horrible details, as the traumatic experience of seeing my son after his death would surely leave deeper wounds to my psyche.

Thursday morning, in the hotel where we were staying, the coroner called to explain his findings. "Ms. Bates, we were able to do a preliminary autopsy. Anthony had a condition called Idiopathic Hypertrophic Subaortic Stenosis (IHSS), also known as Hypertrophic Cardiomyopathy or HCM. Do you have other family members that have died young from a heart condition or for no apparent reason? You should all be screened for this condition, too. We will be listing Anthony's death as "natural death" and be returning his body to Manhattan for your services." This information was so foreign to me. "Screened," what does that mean? "HCM," I had never heard of such a condition, nor understood that heart disease had hereditary factors.

"Natural death?" How is it "natural" for a seemingly healthy twenty-year-old young man to die from this or any heart condition? We later found heart diseases could be detected with Echocardiogram/ Ultrasound and Electrocardiogram (ECG/EKG) screening tests to prevent sudden cardiac arrest and death. In hours of readings and searches on the internet, I came to learn a lot about HCM.

HCM – Hypertrophic Cardiomyopathy

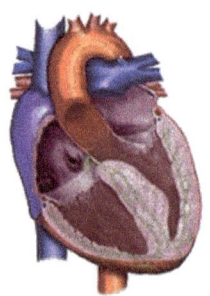
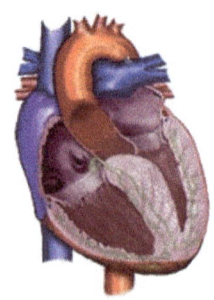

Hypertrophic Cardiomyopathy without obstruction

Hypertrophic Cardiomyopathy with obstruction

Photo courtesy of HCMA

The heart's primary abnormality in Hypertrophic Cardiomyopathy (HCM) is an excessive thickening of the muscle. The distribution of muscle thickening or hypertrophy is variable. The left ventricle is usually affected, and in some patients, the right ventricle tissue thickens.

Asymmetric Septal Hypertrophy

Also called hypertrophic cardiomyopathy, asymmetric septal hypertrophy is thickening of the heart walls in the lower chambers or ventricles (the squeezing part or blood pump of the heart muscle.) The interior and outer walls become thick and the heart becomes inefficient for relaxing to fill the chambers with blood and to pump the blood out to the body. Children with Asymmetric Septal Hypertrophy are more susceptible to Sudden Cardiac Arrest and Death. Therefore, restricting a child from athletics is to protect the child and family from a possible tragedy.

There are no particular symptoms or complaints, which are unique to Hypertrophic Cardiomyopathy (HCM.) Some symptoms may occur at any stage in a person's life, even though the condition may have been present. The reason for the onset of symptoms is often not apparent.

Symptoms of HCM can vary or be completely absent:
- Shortness of Breath
- Chest Pain
- Palpitations (racing heart)
- Dizziness or Fainting
- Extreme Fatigue

What is SCA - Sudden Cardiac Arrest?

The Difference between Sudden Cardiac Arrest and a Heart Attack

Sudden Cardiac Arrest is often confused with a heart attack. Although a prior heart attack increases one's risk for sudden cardiac arrest, the two are quite different, with distinct risk factors, treatment options, and outcomes.

Photo courtesy of Sudden Cardiac Arrest Foundation

Anatomy of a Heart Attack

A circulation problem causes a heart attack when one or more of the arteries delivering blood to the heart are blocked. Oxygen in the blood cannot reach the heart muscle, and the heart muscle becomes damaged. You can think of a heart attack as a "plumbing problem" in the heart.

This damage to the heart muscle can lead to disturbances in the heart's electrical system. Also, a malfunction of the heart's electrical system may cause dangerously fast heart rhythms that can lead to sudden cardiac arrest.

Anatomy of Sudden Cardiac Arrest

In contrast to a heart attack, sudden cardiac arrest is caused by an "electrical problem" in the heart. It occurs when the heart's lower chambers (ventricles) suddenly develop a rapid, irregular rhythm (ventricular fibrillation), causing the ventricles to quiver rather than contract. The ventricles' chaotic quivering motion renders the heart an ineffective pump that can no longer supply the body and brain with oxygen.

Within seconds, the person loses consciousness and has no pulse. Only immediate emergency treatment can prevent death from sudden cardiac arrest. Utilizing Cardiopulmonary Resuscitation (CPR) and Automatic External Defibrillation is helpful in survival. **Time is the key to surviving a sudden cardiac arrest**, with chances of survival decreasing about 10 percent every minute without defibrillation. The American Heart Association (AHA) recommends defibrillation within five minutes of collapse or sooner.

I learned a lot about hearts and heart conditions after Anthony died. That first year was a whirlwind of activities, learning new terms, and making new connections. I was so overwhelmed. There was so much information to sift through, absorb, and comprehend during this monumental task of understanding the disease that took my son's life and to protect my family from any subsequent sudden deaths. There were many sleepless nights in front of my computer screen. I would spend hours reading articles and medical journals during the day. Not being from a medical background, taking on this deep dive of vast information was arduous. I filled many days with tears of frustration and fits of anger. This was especially true when I found the decade's worth of medical studies by the American Heart Association (AHA) and National Football League (NFL) dating into the early 1960s that dealt with Sudden Cardiac Arrest (SCA.) How could these experts bury decades of research studies uncovering the facts about heart conditions leading to SCA, and the circumstances around hundreds of thousands of deaths related to hidden heart issues? Children were dying, and more needed to be done to protect young people at risk of SCA and early death from these heart ailments. I couldn't wait for the government to mandate change. I had to act!

I found it very valuable to understand the information taught to medical professionals. By 2003, I would find myself included at an exhibitor booth at medical conferences. Over the years, I have collected my "name badges" from many medical and educational conferences I have attended, presented, and later hosted through Parent Heart Watch. Knowledge is power and can save future generations of children around the world.

In 2003, I produced my first educational video, "What is HCM?" Even though this was small scale, the process of this problematic production had many delays, additional expenses, and unclear communication challenges. My own experience of just that endeavor could take up another chapter or a small book. It was painful and costly. The videographer seemed like a trustworthy person to embark on this little project. However, I soon became aware that he was the first of many people attempting to take advantage of this grieving mother; I learned from this experience. I guarded myself as I moved forward on my "grief journey." Always get a clear and concise contract with details of all expected expenditures — explanations outlined in the agreement, when changes occur to the project, and additional costs are involved.

After the project was complete, the Anthony Bates Foundation (ABF) made dozens of copies of the short VHS videotapes to distribute to cardiologists in the Phoenix area and other parts of the country. Education and awareness of heart disease in children are among the core values of the ABF Mission Statement. Over time, ABF was able to transfer the production from VHS tapes to DVDs. In our attempt to educate cardiologists, we found six doctors who would help ABF with our screening efforts.

Anthony Bates Foundation (ABF) Mission Statement

"The Anthony Bates Foundation (ABF) believes that no parent should suffer the heartbreak of losing a child to an undiagnosed cardiac malady; we seek to eliminate preventable Sudden Cardiac Arrest (SCA). The organization will fulfill its mission by continuing our efforts to establish a nationwide heart-screening program for youth, free of charge or low cost, thus solving a significant public health issue through screenings, education, collaboration, and facilitation.

ABF is the ONLY organization screening our nation's youth with a copyrighted training protocol and a collection mechanism of epidemiological data that provides valuable information for researchers and medical professionals."

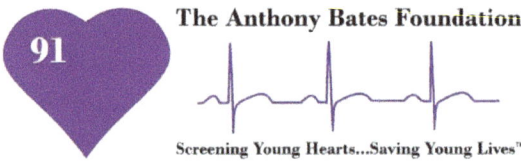

CHAPTER FIVE

My Childhood

I was a teenager, on my own, at the very young age of sixteen. I left my mother's home because her then-husband, Jim, was a sexually abusive stepfather. Three years prior, he had started abusing my two sisters and me. He was a sexual pedophile and preyed upon my older sister, Brenda, my younger sister, Teresa, and me. While my mother worked nights, my stepfather would groom us with gifts or extra treats. He would use the "gifts" to lure one of us into his bedroom for "special massage" time. He included inappropriate touching during his "special massages." My stepbrother, Jimmy, also abused my sisters and me. He would fondle us in the middle of the night in each of our beds. He was not as blatant and aggressive in his pedophile behaviors, as was my stepfather. If I woke up and rolled over, he would stop and leave my room. I am not sure how many times he took advantage of my sisters or me. I found out years later; there was at least one occasion when my younger sister, Teresa, complained to our mother in the middle of the night. Our mother just told her to go back to bed. The next day, neither my sister nor my mother said anything about that incident.

The abuse went on for several months when I finally took a stand. I was thirteen years old; I stood up to the two pedophiles by speaking the truth to my mother. I made my accusations of the abuse to her, not realizing my younger sister, Teresa, had tried to sound the alarm earlier. The same abuse from our stepbrother happened to Teresa, and my mother didn't believe either of us. On the other hand, maybe she didn't want to consider us as truthful. When I spoke up, I told my mother that my stepfather had done bad things to my older sister, Brenda, and me. But, when my mother confronted Brenda about the abuse, Brenda would not confirm them. She denied it to my mother and ignored me. Years later, I learned the reason behind her denial.

Brenda felt guilty about a previous experience when she was a small, five-year-old child. Edna, my mother, and all three of my sisters and I were waiting in the car for my biological father, Larry, who was having a beer in a bar with his friends while we waited. Brenda and my mother were in the front seat; my other sisters, Teresa and Diane, and I played in the back seat. Brenda uncovered a piece of paper in the glove box. She showed it to our mother. The "paper" turned out to be a hotel receipt proving our father was having an affair. That discovery led to our parent's divorce, and my sister never forgave herself. She was just a child, though, and not to blame.

After I spoke the truth of my stepfather's and stepbrother's abuses, my mother continued to reject my "story" because my older sister would not corroborate the accusations. I didn't realize Brenda was holding such guilt for our mother's first marriage failure. After many tear-filled days and nights that summer of 1975, my mother contacted our biological father. By the end of June, my mother sent me to Alameda, California, to spend some time with my biological father, Larry Foote. He was stationed there in the Navy. By this time, Larry was remarried and had two children. For obvious reasons, the trip was not pleasant.

After a few weeks with my father's new family, I confided in him about the sexual abuse I was receiving. It turned out he did not believe me, either. His words were shocking to me as a thirteen-year-old girl.

In disbelief, he said to me, "What do you want me to do?"

My first thoughts were, *"You are my father! You are an adult! You are supposed to protect me!"*

I'm not exactly sure what I said, though. Probably something like, "I don't know!" Through all those tears, I knew I needed to get back home to protect my sisters from the sexual pedophiles in our home in Coquitlam, British Columbia, Canada. I had to stand up for the truth, and know my inner strength. However, I was still a child myself. What could I do?

I went back home to Canada to protect my sisters, or so I thought. Instead of returning a hero, I came home to three angry sisters. They ganged up on me to shame me for the truth that I told. They called me a "prostitute" and a "whore," but I do not even think my two younger sisters, Teresa and Diane, even knew what those words meant. Over a few months, things seemed to settle back into a normal process. School had started; my "haven" was available to me once again. However, I was having bad headaches and tearful outbursts regularly, and I could not concentrate, which I had previously been able to do in school. Then, on one occasion, I was babysitting for my stepsister, Bernice. I confided in her about the abuses. Finally, someone believed me. That was indeed a feeling of relief. For a time, I thought I was going crazy. My sisters didn't "have my back" even though I was standing up for them. I felt so alone.

Years would go by with no support and no help from my own family. At least there was no sexual abuse going on anymore. My mother stopped trusting my stepfather. She quit her night waitressing job. She only would work while we were in school. She would not leave us girls alone with those "two pedophiles" at all. Somehow, her actions spoke volumes to me. She never told me that she believed me. However, by her actions, the truth was revealed. Before she married our stepfather in 1970, we were living in poverty. Looking back on my childhood, I didn't realize our situation was so impoverished. Our mother's meager wages and tips as a "food server" didn't go far. The child support my mother received from our father was only $100 per month for four children. It didn't cover the cost of food and lodging, let alone any extras. We had little food to eat, nowhere pleasant to live, and had to stay in various homes with roommates to help make ends meet. We had little support from our father, which must have led my mother to accept our stepfather's marriage offer. Her only mechanism to protect her children was to put herself between the pedophiles and her girls without ending up on the street.

When I turned fifteen, my mother and stepfather had returned from a vacation in Phoenix, Arizona. They had a wild idea that they

17

would move to the States. Auntie Bernice Long, our stepfather's sister, lived in Phoenix. There was a job waiting for my stepfather, and the economy was better in the States. On the other hand, he could have been running away from a possible conviction for sex crimes. Unfortunately, even in Canada, the laws were not as strict against pedophiles as they are now.

There was a family meeting early in 1977. Our parents said that we would all need to pool our money for the move to be successful. What kind of crazy idea would that be? I had a few hundred dollars in the bank from my babysitting, Christmas and birthday money. I wasn't about to share that with HIM! Plus, I had plans for my education, and I had friends at school. I didn't want to move. I wasn't alone in that feeling, as my older sister, Brenda, didn't want to move. My sisters and I were all angry and sad about the potential move. The possibility of leaving Canada was an enormous emotional upheaval for us teenage girls. My sisters and I had never been to Phoenix, and all our friends were in Canada. It was devastating for us.

Even under duress, moving started, and we had to pack up our rooms and belongings. But, what hurts my heart the most was when my parents decided to put down our dogs. At that time, we had five dogs. My parents decided to bring the two poodles with us to Arizona. Their reasoning was small dogs were easier to transport. Two of the others were German Shepherd dogs, and third was a German Short Haired Pointer. These three dogs were older and possibly not the easiest to be re-homed. It just didn't seem like my parents even tried to find new homes for our dogs. Euthanizing family pets was such a bad experience and not a good lesson for young people. In my opinion, these actions serve as another example of inappropriate behavior by my mother and stepfather.

It was a long drive, in the moving truck caravan, to Phoenix in August of 1977. We made it in about three days. Seven of the ten family members packed the truck with our family's belongings and moved to Phoenix. The three adult stepsisters stayed in Canada with their growing families. The only advantage of that move is that our new house had a swimming pool. That is a considerable advantage during the sweltering Arizona summers.

Then school started once again, and we had to walk to and from school, which was more than a mile each way in the Arizona heat. We were able to cut through Cortez Park on the way to Cortez High School. There was a fishing pond with dozens of ducks to amuse us before and after school. The morning walks were pleasant, but the afternoon Arizona heat in August was brutal. With our chores and homework completed, we took advantage of the swimming pool.

Early into my experience of the U.S. schools, my world came crashing down. There was a considerable difference between the U.S. and Canada education systems. I was shocked that, as a sophomore in high school, the classes were way behind Canada's courses. The Algebra classes in the U.S. were two years behind my previous Canadian courses. My delayed Canadian transcripts led to an ineffective complaint to my guidance counselor. My mother didn't bring the paperwork with her to enroll us in school. Disappointed, I had to wait. When the transcripts arrived in November, it was too late to switch to the higher learning classes. I was devastated and angry once again.

The first Christmas in the States brought me some relief. Somehow, my older sister, Brenda, decided to confess the sex abuse episodes in Canada. She told me when she was five years old and found the hotel's receipt of our father's affair. That discussion was when we became true sisters, and from then on, we "had each other's backs." She had been just a little girl and carried the weight of her unfortunate discovery on her shoulders. I became angrier and more distant from my mother.

Shortly after the holidays, my Auntie Bernice found out about my plight. In early 1978, she stormed into our house after learning of my accusations and confronted her brother, my stepfather, Jim. There was yelling, arguing, and she was very emotional. Her father, my step-grandfather, had abused my Auntie Bernice as a little girl. The abuse cycle continued in this family.

During the confrontation, my three sisters and I stayed in our rooms. In total dismay, my mother burst into my bedroom that day and said the same thing my father said to me in 1975, *"What am I supposed to do?"*

My instant thoughts, *"Ugh, why do I always have to be the adult in this family?"*

I told my mother not to worry, "I will be moving out!"

By that time, I had a job, and a boyfriend, Joe, and I went to live with him. We were a young, naive couple taking on the world. We got married about three months after the birth of our son, Anthony. Joe and I were together for two years, but our marriage didn't last a year. Growing up is hard to do, especially when you have a baby at 17 and get married for the wrong reasons.

CHAPTER SIX

ABF Beginnings

Back at Kansas State University, to help with their grief over Anthony's loss, I connected with the players, university employees, and coaches. Before Anthony died, I would travel to Kansas to visit him, and I would bring him a suitcase full of goodies, gifts, and local foods. After his death, I did the same for the football players, staff, and coaches. They were all grieving, and I needed to provide some nurturing support for them, and secretly for myself.

I wanted each of the players and staff to have a token or memento to remember Anthony. When we cleaned out Anthony's  apartment, he had a collection of old movies that used to belong to his step-grandfather. One of the K-State football team captains, Jason

Kazar, mentioned during Anthony's funeral about Anthony's ability to quote movie lines and make the other football team members chuckle or laugh. With permission from the football office, I set up a small event in the Big 12 Room at the Kansas State University football complex. During my trip to Kansas, to clean out Anthony's apartment, I displayed his belongings to gift to his teammates after football practice. As the players cleaned up after their workout, Head Football Coach Bill Snyder stopped by and checked in on me. The coach was always so caring and supportive of me, but the coaches and

Anthony's teammates were also grieving. He even created a temporary memorial out of Anthony's locker to allow the players to hold Anthony in their hearts. The team decided to wear a large sticker on each helmet's back with the number "91," representing Anthony's jersey number. In the early days of my "grief journey," Coach Snyder shared touching heartfelt words and support that gave me strength. Several years later, Coach Snyder created a permanent memorial outside of the football complex for Anthony Bates, Troy Miller, Bob Cope, and Nancy Bennett. Each tragically lost their lives during Coach Snyder's era. I am grateful to have offered some peace and comfort to the Kansas State University Football team during their own "grief journey" that overlapped mine.

As I searched through the internet, I found the Hypertrophic Cardiomyopathy Association (HCMA) and connected with Lisa Salberg, HCMA President and Founder, to learn about the disease. We connected and became fast friends during my grief journey. Lisa was very knowledgeable about HCM as well as her own "grief journey." She openly shared information with me, as I was attempting to understand a heart condition that could be a danger to numerous family members. Lisa had lost five family members to the disease that ravages families with little or no warning.

On the internet, shortly after Anthony's death, Allen Bates, Anthony's adopted father, found Chuck Morrell. Chuck was a former college and NFL football player who connected us to his daughter, Holly. She was Executive Director of A Heart for Sports (AHFS) and now the founder of Heartfelt Cardiac Project. Holly taught me a lot about heart-screenings. After Holly and Chuck lost six family members, including cousins, uncles, and grandparents to HCM, they advocated and organized heart-screenings for youth and families.

Holly's father, Chuck, had HCM and received a heart transplant five years before we met. Chuck was a passionate advocate of the benefit to early detection of HCM and the prevention of Sudden Cardiac Death on the playing field. He lived about ten years post-transplant and was a significant influence in his daughter's life and my efforts to screen young hearts. Many people miss Chuck; almost everyone who knew him loved him.

Seaneen and Jeff Greaves founded A Heart for Sports (AHFS) in Loma Linda, California. Holly Morrell was their Executive Director in the early years. Their organization was the first of two I discovered to be hosting youth cardiac screenings. AHFS was in Southern California close to Phoenix, but not New Jersey. At that time, I wasn't sure how I could make a significant contribution to my son's memory, but I knew that something big was in store for my life. Why not save as many young lives as I could to honor Anthony? Holly was helpful and supportive of whatever my desires were in saving young lives. Our symbiotic friendship blossomed as the months rolled on.

It turns out that Lisa Salberg and her organization, HCMA were in Hibernia, New Jersey, a short drive from Little Ferry. Lisa taught me a lot about these heart issues and the health issues that people with HCM deal within their lives. For our first screening at Kansas State University, she allowed me to use the Hypertrophic Cardiomyopathy Association (HCMA) non-profit umbrella. That way, the donations we received would be tax-deductible. At first, this made it a lot easier than starting my foundation. Besides, I was still living in New Jersey and unsure if I would ever start a foundation in my son's name.

At age twelve, Lisa and her older sister, Lori, were diagnosed with HCM. Additionally, many of Lisa's family members received HCM diagnoses. They were all stricken with this chronic disease and living with HCM. A few years before Anthony died, Lisa's sister succumbed, at age thirty-six, to HCM, mainly due to her medical providers mishandled her care. Lisa fought back by creating the HCMA to honor her sister and to help countless families traverse the healthcare "minefields" of living with this chronic illness, with individualized symptoms and outcomes. Not every doctor on this planet has the expertise to help people transverse the minefields of an unique and strange manifestation of this heart disease. At the time of Anthony's death, experts reported that one in 500 people in the general populous had or were at risk of developing HCM in their lifetime. In 2016, those figures rose to one in 250 people who could have HCM. Lisa continues today to build a national string of HCM Centers of Excellence for the medical professionals to treat people with this condition. I will always be grateful to Lisa for her knowledge and advocacy. I will also be forever thankful to the HCM community for its support and encouragement over these twenty years and counting.

Holly Morrell connected me to Arista Butrum, who had founded the Chad Foundation for Artists and Athletes from New York, New York. Arista lost her son, Chad, from Dilated Cardiomyopathy (DCM.) Experts suspect that DCM is the end-stages of HCM. DCM attacks the whole heart, thinning all the heart walls and weakening its function; whereas, HCM attacks the left side of the heart muscle, thickening the walls and reducing blood flow to the body. Arista's son died, in 1996, at age twenty-eight from undiagnosed DCM. Both Arista and Holly had the first community screening programs in the U.S. I was amazed by their enthusiasm to provide such an excellent service. Soon after our meeting, I realized there were tremendous roadblocks to developing a thriving national heart-screening program.

In late 2000, I met Linette Derminer from Geneva, Ohio, through an internet search. Her son, Ken, died to undiagnosed HCM in June 2000, a few short weeks before Anthony died. Linette and her husband, Mark, started a foundation in honor of their son. The foundation was called Kids Endangered Now, (KEN). We connected through emails and numerous phone calls. She was keeping track of the stories in the media of children who were dying. Linette started this effort after her son's doctor explained that HCM deaths were rare, and she would probably never hear of another case. The exact opposite was true. Three weeks after her son Ken died, another young man died just a few towns from her in Ohio. Riddled with disbelief that another tragedy struck again, Linette started building the first database of young lives lost with death reasons. She was able to find out the causes of death beyond "natural" to the real reasons children were dying -- heart diseases!

Years later, a group of research doctors used Linette's database. These doctors proved and validated the number of young deaths in our country due to Sudden Cardiac Arrest (SCA). Linette provided endless hours of uncompensated work on her database used in the research study, which launched additional models for other research. I am grateful to her tenacity and exposure of the truth that children are dying in our country in high numbers.

Another mother, Rachel Moyer, connected us all. In late 2000, Rachel and her husband, John, lost their son, Gregory, to HCM. They created the Gregory W. Moyer Defibrillator Fund from Shawnee on Delaware, Pennsylvania. Gregory had collapsed at halftime in the locker room during a basketball game. At the time of his collapse, the team trainer and coaches waited for the EMTs to arrive. There was no Automatic External Defibrillator (AED) available, and no one did CPR on Greg. All of our grief-stricken families were advocating for the same things: better tracking of Sudden Cardiac Death (SCD); mandating at the state and school district level for Automatic External Defibrillators (AEDs) in schools; and advocating for mandatory heart-screenings for children.

On many occasions, these women and I would have lengthy phone conversations and multiple emails regarding uncovering reports of previous sudden cardiac arrest studies. Together we were on a mission to save lives! Our passion was over-flowing because of our love for our children and all the world's children. We supported each other in our "grief journey" and tried to save the lives of vulnerable children.

On one of my numerous trips back to Manhattan, Kansas, I told Coach Bill Snyder about Holly and her screening program. He said to me, "Sharon, you need to do the screenings. You have the story and the connection to K-State." That is how Coach Snyder encouraged me to create the Anthony Bates Foundation (ABF). Anthony had taught me, "When your coach tells you to do something, it must be done."

In September 2001, the California screening Holly had hosted turned out to be big and exciting. Philips Medical was a sponsor and did a big media blitz, too. I learned about controlling the media, heart-screenings, echo stations, and the flow of participants. I was curious and had many questions for the founders of A Heart for Sports, Seaneen and Jeff Greaves. Unfortunately, they were not available after the screening event to offer support. The amount of energy it takes to put on such an event was new to me. However, from the event experiences, I vowed to help as many people as possible to create screenings in the U.S.

A few weeks later, the second screening I attended was also in California. Arista and the Chad Foundation hosted their screening event during a charity volleyball tournament on Malibu's beaches. In attendance were Gabby Reece, the world-famous volleyball player, and several hundred spectators. There was a large tent to screen a few dozen people. The perspective of this event allowed me to visualize various ways to offer these life-saving screening tests. Heart-Screening events are not "cookie-cutter" programs. Each event is unique for different communities and circumstances. Sharing the program style is the first step, and allowing the organizers to make the heart-screening event match the particular area becomes the magic.

Our first several years of screenings in the ABF program provided ultrasound and blood pressure tests only. Blood pressure was simple to produce, with a few automatic blood pressure kits purchased from the local drug stores. We borrowed echo machines from the sales representatives of the various manufacturers: Siemens Medical Solutions, Philips Medical, General Electric Medical, and Sonosite. With only three heart-screening organizations hosting screenings in our country, asking for access to ultrasound equipment on the weekend was not an issue. The ultrasound manufacturers met our requests with open arms. It turns out that the sales representatives were able to display new machines to our attending doctors and ultrasound technicians. In the beginning, everyone won in this scenario.

The challenges I faced at the time of Anthony's death were multifaceted. The computer work slowed at Bridan Technologies in Saddlebrook, New Jersey, where I was employed. Technology took a hit on the prosperity wheel after Y2K sputtered out. Then I faced the realization that Anthony was not a child from New Jersey; he was born in Flagstaff, Arizona, and raised in Phoenix, Arizona, and Wichita, Kansas. Where could I make the most significant impact to honor his memory? It didn't seem like New Jersey was the best location to create a foundation or program in Anthony's honor.

By early 2001, I decided to move back to Phoenix and start Anthony's foundation. I would help educate the public and bring about awareness of heart disease in children, screening youth, and building a volunteer-based program where many people would know his name and remember his legacy. Unfortunately, my fiancé, Steve, did not want to move to Phoenix, and we ended our relationship. Ninety percent of marriages fail after the loss of a child; this is a sad statistic. There does not seem to be a statistic for unmarried couples or relationships. Over the years, many people have slipped away, or the dynamics of these relationships changed. Some have evolved into close friendships. However, often the stress of change doesn't fit well with some people.

Shortly after I moved back to Phoenix, I started back in computer consulting to have part-time work that would allow me to focus my other time on educating children about heart disease. One of the first jobs I took on was working with the third-largest school district in Arizona, Peoria Unified School District (PUSD) in Peoria, Arizona. The district Business Manager was my former computer-consulting colleague, Sandy Wilkins. Sandy interacted with Anthony when he was alive and empathized with my pain after he died. Sandy brought me into PUSD to support some custom computer program needs at the school district. Several years earlier, when our Bates family moved to Arizona in 1990, Sandy and I worked together through Computer Software Corporation and Maricopa County Schools. For practical purposes, putting back the old team to work on projects was a godsend for Sandy and me. We both got what we needed through our business connection and some much-needed support in our healing.

My previous experiences working with schools came in handy for my future job, running a non-profit. I had been a past PTA President for Chisholm Elementary School in Wichita, Kansas. I had been Anthony's Cub Scout Webelo Den Leader and a Boy Scout parent supporting him through earning his Eagle Scout by age fifteen. Later on, when Anthony got to high school, I volunteered for Anthony's Football Booster Club at Mountain Pointe High School. That progressed into my two-year term as Booster President. All the years of my involvement helped train me for the most relevant job of my life, CEO/Founder of the Anthony Bates Foundation (ABF.)

Genuine empathy and altruism arose in me during these volunteer experiences. Giving back to my town, community, city, state, and the country was so enriching. In Anthony's training to become an Eagle Scout, the philosophy was always, "Since the earliest days of Scouting; Scouts have worked to make the world a better place." How could I do anything less? Volunteerism was the way to build a cost-effective program for the masses. Where does one start? I was willing to "try my own backyard" or the "next yard over" in Southern California, not far from Arizona.

CHAPTER SEVEN

Screening through the Grief

Through the months and years after Anthony's death, I learned a lot about the left side of a heart where HCM usually develops and a lot about my need to give back to the world. The internet was a blessing and a curse for searching to understand Anthony's death. However, not everything on the internet seemed to be what it was. Some of the research items were not valid. Some of the paths I traveled were dead ends. Not everyone I found on the internet could lead me to answers. There are always things on the internet that were just not true, somewhat misleading, and sometimes just scams. That is true even in today's internet. Fortunately, I could sift through much of the falsehoods and get to the truth and find the right people, even when it wasn't easy.

Within months after Anthony died, I had renewed energy that carried me through the next five years, and my soul was filled with enthusiasm, as my life had goals. I felt I was living for a purpose, to "screen young hearts and save young lives!" We organized seventeen heart-screening events and screened 3,071 young hearts, finding

190 problems (six percent) with sixty of those tested to be "Possible Life-Threatening" (two-percent) problems.

By 2002, the Anthony Bates Foundation (ABF) became an official 501(c)(3). A non-profit organization must have this IRS designation to allow our donor's tax deductions on their income tax forms for their charitable contributions. Giving back to the communities we serve allows ABF tax breaks on our tax-forms as well. The community wins, and we are allowed to operate as a not-for-profit corporation. Through the Mom's Team (Rachel, Linette, and me), we created our first collaborative organization, The National Coalition of Parents Network. In 2005, Laura Friend from North Richland Hills, Texas, joined our influence network. Laura and her husband, Luther's daughter, Sarah, died in 2004 from HCM. We met Laura at the HCMA conference in early 2005. Laura had already created a successful 5K fundraiser and organization Run for Sarah, and could benefit our Mom's team with her expertise and passion. In July 2005, all four grieving mothers, Rachel, Linette, Laura, and I, traveled to Las Vegas to meet with Medtronic Foundation, our founding partner. We were allowed to create what is today, Parent Heart Watch (PHW). Joan Mellor, Medtronic Foundation employee and one of several champions within that foundation, arranged the meeting in Las Vegas to start this collaboration.

Later that same year, with a small grant from the Medtronic Foundation, I created my first edition of "How to Host Community Cardiac Screening Events." I had conversations with Holly regarding the creation of a community screening training manual. We had both received numerous emails and phone calls from other desperate grieving families. They searched for a "how-to" guide or screening manual or just wanted us to reply to their email with all the answers that would help them build a program of their own. How could we respond to an email regarding all we knew about putting together a screening event? Each event is different, and every community has its challenges. There had to be a more natural way to support families searching for a program that would honor their child. In my computer career, I had experience creating manuals supporting software updates and user interfaces. It made sense for me to put together the first "how-to" manual.

Parent Heart Watch (PHW) was a fledgling organization. I was on their first board of directors from 2005 until 2009. As the organization grew, the board responsibilities became more time-consuming. ABF and I needed to focus on our heart-screening and the ABF Training Program, "How to Host Community Cardiac Screening Events." From the initial onset of PHW, the primary funding sources were the Automatic External Defibrillator (AED) manufacturers and personal donations. As PHW grew, the sad reality was that more parents joined the organization because they had lost a child from Sudden Cardiac Arrest (SCA). The initial efforts of most parents were to honor their child that died. Small fundraisers would allow parents the ability to donate an AED to their child's school. There were many times that schools would deny such a donation, as the liability would be significant if only one school in the district was protected and the other schools were not. PHW parents in our states and around the country took on the challenge. They did more great work to protect all children from SCA with Automatic External Defibrillator (AED) placement and Emergency Preparedness Plans (EPP).

Several of the AED Manufacturers would send sales representatives to the Parent Heart Watch annual meetings. Initially, I was not interested in AED placement for the schools' ABF Heart-Screenings. However, I created several great relationships and friendships in the AED circle of influence. Jonathan Rittenburg lived in Scottsdale, Arizona, and was the territory manager for Cardiac Science. He was able to attend the first PHW annual meeting in Las Vegas, Nevada. He shared with me, on several occasions, the passion that was in that room during the first meeting. Jonathan was a tireless advocate for protecting children and families from Sudden Cardiac Death. I will be forever grateful to Jonathan, the shared meals and contacts, and the support he gave to ABF and PHW.

The Cardiac Science Global Director of Marketing, Al Ford, was also at the first Parent Heart Watch meeting. On several occasions at the PHW annual meetings, Al and I would cross paths. He was always advocating to protect children, families, and communities from Sudden Cardiac Death. He recently shared with me, "I always thought it was a no-brainer that people would grasp onto AED placements' protection measures in schools. However, nineteen years in the business made me realize the opposite." We shared our passion and wisdom for saving young lives through our support and struggles that created real friendships. I am forever grateful to these two men and many in the business that helped ABF and PHW.

By 2006, the Parent Heart Watch (PHW) leadership, and I made several in-roads on the medical conference circuit. News spread across the country that we were leaders and members of PHW, strategically covering the nation. Having advocates and parents spread across the country was to our advantage. When dates were announced for medical and sports safety conferences, the PHW Board would determine the importance of attendance and reach the local members for additional support. On several occasions, I would travel to represent PHW and ABF. That same year, I was an exhibitor in Philadelphia, Pennsylvania, at the Cardiology Conference. Children's Hospital of Philadelphia and Dr. Vicki Vetter, Pediatric Cardiologist, and PHW Medical Board of Advisor hosted the conference. After Rachel Moyer and I shared some screening insights with Dr. Vetter over dinner, Dr. Vetter became a colossal proponent supporting heart-screenings for youth and a "Heart Champion."

In 2007, I attended the American Society of Echocardiography (ASE) in Seattle, Washington. Seattle was also the home of Dr. Jonathan Drezner. In 2006, he and I had crossed paths at the "Prevention of Sudden Cardiac Death in Athletes" conference in Jackson, Mississippi. Dr. Drezner and his team are true "Heart Champions" for PHW and the heart-screening programs nationwide. His team of doctors has authored several medical studies, including the "Seattle Criteria[2]," and they have become outspoken advocates of heart-screenings in our nation.

While I attended the Seattle conference in 2007, I connected with Darla Varrenti and her sister, Suzanne Apodaca, who lived in the Seattle area. In 2004, Darla lost her son, Nicky, to undiagnosed HCM.

---

[2]   Electrocardiographic interpretation in athletes: the 'Seattle Criteria,' Authors: Jonathan A Drezner,1Michael John Ackerman, Jeffrey Anderson, Euan Ashley, Chad A Asplund, Aaron L Baggish, Mats Börjesson, Bryan C Cannon, Domenico Corrado, John P DiFiori, Peter Fischbach, Victor Froelicher, Kimberly G Harmon, Hein Heidbuchel, Joseph Marek, David S Owens, Stephen Paul, Antonio Pelliccia, Jordan M Prutkin, Jack C Salerno, Christian M Schmied, Sanjay Sharma, Ricardo Stein, Victoria L Vetter, Mathew G Wilson, Publication: bsmj.bsm.com, Date: January 10, 2013

Although they were new on their grief journey, Darla, Suzanne, and her husband, Steve, attended the inaugural PHW meeting in 2005. By 2007, this family wanted to make a mark on SCA in their community. I invited the women to participate in the conference to network with the medical professionals in their community who attended this conference. That was the start of something great. Shortly after my visit, Darla and Suzanne decided to start screening through their newly formed organization, Nick of Time Foundation, a.k.a. "NoT."

I was able to put Darla and Suzanne in touch with Dr. Drezner and doctors at Seattle Children's Hospital. Almost immediately, the team started devising plans to heart screen in Seattle. As a new ABF Trained Team, NoT quickly learned a lot, and were enthusiastic to "screen young hearts and save young lives!" We worked together in support of the first heart-screening event in Seattle. ABF would provide much of the equipment and secure some borrowed equipment from within the community. NoT would work in the community to ensure the event location and many of the volunteers. Jointly, we invited doctors and medical professionals to volunteer their services for the upcoming heart-screening event. To make the heart-screening more exciting, PHW planned its 2008 conference in Seattle. We were able to showcase a heart-screening event while training families and medical professionals in the life-saving program. To this day, the Nick of Time Foundation (NoT) is a leader in the heart-screening industry and amazes me with their strength and endurance. They are real "Heart Champions."

In 2013, Parent Heart Watch (PHW) returned to Seattle for another annual meeting. At this event, the University of Washington conducted a medical continuing-education component with a Certificate of Equivalent Experience (CEE), hosted by Dr. Drezner, his team and the Nick of Time Foundation. During the PHW annual meeting, I sat in the back of the room with several parents and long-time friends. By this meeting, I had thirteen years of medical education and heard a lot of rhetoric. However, this time, Dr. Kimberly Harmon was giving a presentation that caught my attention. She was punching holes in the long-time research and erroneous conclusions of Dr. Barry Maron that had held back the medical community for years, from taking action to stop SCA. Doctors would not get involved in heart-screenings events because of Dr. Maron's flawed study, which concluded that there was no "scientific data" proving heart-screenings' value. Dr. Harmon and the NoT Foundation had data, and her presence made my heart sing with joy, as tears fill my eyes. Hallelujah, the rest of the medical professionals, now had proof that screenings were saving lives!

I stepped out of the conference room to find some more tissues to dry my eyes. I ran into Laura Friend, the fourth co-founder of Parent Heart Watch. She stopped me short. "What's wrong, Sharon?" I took a moment to realize that she hadn't been in the room to hear the exciting presentation. I explained, "Oh Laura, it's like the tides have turned, and the troops have been sent in to fight for our kids!" I will never forget that conference and the excitement that our medical professionals began doing to help blaze the trail in this effort to "screen young hearts and save young lives!" I am forever grateful to each "Heart Champion" who has blazed a trail toward eliminating preventable Sudden Cardiac Arrest in children!

Everyone had a "little bump" in the road (which for far too many was a "major crash") with the 2008 recession. From 2009 until 2012, donations were down, and activities slowed our services to the communities. However, a recession does not stop Sudden Cardiac Arrest from taking its deadly toll. The sad truth about heart disease is that it kills more people globally than any other cause of death. Annually over 17 million people die from cardiovascular disease, which is way more than all other death causes combined. Therefore, countries, states, communities, and regions were searching for solutions to this global problem.

Schools were looking for new ways to receive the life-saving equipment. In 2011, that is when I created the "ABF Heart Screens for AEDs." By 2013, Peoria Unified School District and Apache Junction School District in Arizona, allowed ABF to help their schools place AEDs in the elementary schools. Within eighteen months, ABF completed the project in both districts. We had raised the needed funds, placed the AEDs in the schools, trained the staff to protect the students, and we screened over 1000 young hearts. In those events, we discovered 203 people with heart issues, of which thirty-nine were "Possible Life-Threatening" issues, which means we saved the lives of thirty-nine people. ABF wrote several grant proposals and received rewards that allowed ABF to complete the project sooner. We purchased and donated forty AEDs, and the school districts purchased six additional AEDs. Subsequently, ABF provided CPR and AED training to over 350 staff for these districts.

A few years earlier, I attended one of those numerous medical conferences. This one was held in Chicago in October 2009 for the Sudden Cardiac Arrest Association (SCAA) for their annual meeting offering medical education on SCA. The SCAA supports people that have suffered and survived an SCA. The organization also advocates for education and awareness of SCA in our country. I traveled to this conference to represent Parent Heart Watch (PHW) and ABF. I hosted a table with PHW and Anthony Bates Foundation (ABF) materials. All materials were available to share with medical professionals and conference attendees to connect more parents to the work started by four mothers. On several occasions, I had previously met Bob Schriever, Co-founder of SCAA. I was excited to learn more from his team. I would network with other people and groups while learning about some of their conference educational materials. I met another mother who influenced me profoundly. I met this delightful woman, Jackie Renfrow, while she was assisting at the SCAA information table.

While Bob led the conference, meeting with influential SCAA attendees and medical professionals, Jackie and I got to know each other. I shared my story of Anthony and Parent Heart Watch. Then Jackie shared her story of the loss of her children. Her story both horrified and amazed me with her grit, passion, and will to give back to our country but deeply disturbed me because of the lack of knowledge the medical professionals in her area had about SCA. The need to increase understanding of SCA causes was the main reason the invited attendees were medical professionals and SCA Survivors. It was vital for them to continue their education and collaboration on this crucial subject.

Jackie's story was very different from mine in that her family had a history of fainting and seizures. Her mother and sister had fainting spells. Jackie had these spells, too, and so did her daughter and son. In the 1960s, the doctors treated Jackie, her sister, and her mother for epileptic seizures, but that turned out to be a misdiagnosis. Her son, Jimmy, would have seizures, usually in his sleep. When Jackie's son and daughter experienced similar symptoms, their doctors misdiagnosed the children. By April 2000, a few months before Anthony died, Jackie's son, Jimmy, in his early twenties, had reported to his wife that night that he wasn't feeling well. He went to bed early and never woke up. Jimmy died on April 15, 2000. He left a wife with a little girl and no means of support. At no time after Jimmy's death did the doctor's or medical examiner in Indiana recommend further evaluation or testing for the family.

By 2001, Jackie's surviving daughter, Crissy, started her own family and had a daughter. Everything seemed reasonable until a year later, when Crissy had another fainting spell, but she never recovered this time. She died on July 23, 2002, leaving her eight-month-old daughter motherless. Jackie reported to me that at no time after Crissy's death did the doctor's or medical examiner in Indiana recommend further evaluation or testing for the family.

Another ten months after Crissy's death, Jackie's seventy-four-year-old mother had a fainting spell that brought her into the local hospital emergency room. Fortunately, the young doctor asked a few additional questions. When he learned of her grandchildren's deaths, the doctor tending to Jackie's mother ordered a further test of an Electrocardiogram (ECG/EKG). That is when the doctor discovered grandma had Long-QT Syndrome. This electrical problem in the heart can cause Sudden Cardiac Death. Currently, the national average of Long-QT is one in 7,000 people in the general population. The vast twenty-year database of ABF heart-screenings shows Long-QT much higher, at one in 1,875 people screened. Subsequently, the doctors finally diagnosed Long-QT in Jackie, her mother, her sister, and Jimmy and Crissy's two surviving children. To protect their lives, all of Jackie's surviving family members with Long QT received surgery. They would receive the life-saving devices called implanted Internal Cardioverter Defibrillator (ICD).

Jackie continues to advocate for children and families with the Sudden Cardiac Arrest Association Indiana Chapter. She is a huge advocate for educating the public and medical professionals on proper testing for hidden heart issues. Her painful story motivated me to do more and stand up for the children of this country: Thank you, Jackie, for being my role model for courage and perseverance.

My friend, Bob Schriever, also blazed a trail in his efforts to curb Sudden Cardiac Arrest (SCA). Bob was a former college and high-school football and lacrosse official. He also worked for the NFL's New England Patriots as a sideline crew member for more than ten years. On September 14, 2002, Bob, age 61, officiated a high-school football game. During that game, he "died" for more than two and a half minutes.

The visiting team's head athletic trainer had apologized to Bob after arriving late to the game because he had stopped to pick up a newly acquired Automatic External Defibrillator (AED) at his school before the game. Bob would never have imagined that the AED would revive him fifteen minutes into the second half of the game!

After Bob healed from his Sudden Cardiac Arrest (SCA), by 2006 he had connected with other SCA Survivors and form the current Sudden Cardiac Arrest Association (SCAA.) In 2015, I joined the board of the SCAA to become allies with their national program. As I continue to support SCAA, PHW, the ABF Trained Teams, and ABF, I realize all these organizations have a purpose, place, and message to share.

Bob had been involved in a push to help SCA survivors before starting SCAA with his fellow SCA survivors, Jack Grogan and Richard Brown. In 2004, sponsored by Medtronic, Bob and his fellow survivors were advocating, in Washington, D.C., to participate in "Hill Day," which was, at that time, every Wednesday, where organizations with a "cause" could meet with Senators, Congressmen, and Congresswomen on the Hill to advocate for changes. Ahead of time, the sponsor made an appointment for Bob and the group; Bob would then meet Ted Kennedy, his Senator from Massachusetts. At the time, the bill the survivor groups were promoting was about buying Automatic External Defibrillators (AEDs) without a doctor's prescription. Bob's account is below.

Senator Ted Kennedy and Bob Schriever

"When it was our turn to meet with the senator, his secretary showed us into his office. In this meeting, the late Connie Snell was an SCA survivor from Texas with her husband, making it a group of six people. We all sat to await the senator's arrival. Shortly after our entrance, Senator Ted Kennedy and his two dogs entered the room. We stood to greet him. Of course, old-matronly women and dogs seem to like me.

Before we could greet the senator, he remarked to me, "You look familiar . . . I know you! You're the referee that survived the heart attack."

Bob continues, "Yes, I am. But, sir, we did meet once before. When you were running for President, there was a town hall meeting at the South Attleboro Holiday Inn. I had to leave early, and you watched me leave, and our eyes locked for a moment." Bob explained to me that it was as if they knew they would meet again.

Senator Kennedy replied, "I remember."

Bob shared with me that he went into his pitch regarding the AED bill the sponsor had sent the group to discuss. After a few moments, Senator Kennedy picked up the phone and called the head of the FDA. They had a brief conversation; Bob only heard Senator Kennedy's side. "What's holding up the bill to allow AEDs to be purchased without a doctor's prescription?" He was quiet for a moment and then continued, "Oh, is that is all?" They continued on some personal business for about a minute, and then he ended the call.

Senator Kennedy turned to Bob and the group, "You got it! We will add this to the bill."

Then Bob reached into his pocket and retrieved a sample Internal Cardioverter Defibrillator (ICD) and handed it to Senator Kennedy. Bob explained, "I brought this for you. It is an ICD. Surgeons implant these units in the chest of someone who has survived a Sudden Cardiac Arrest. It costs, out of pocket, about $66,000. Not everyone can afford that much."

Bob shared with me that Senator Kennedy listened intently for more than ten minutes. Bob knew his time with the senator was limited, but the senator's secretary gave him a sign to continue. Bob mentioned that Connie Snell had one implanted. Connie invited the senator to see her implant scar by peeling back the corner of her blouse. He approached but hesitated to touch her scar, Connie took his hand, placed it on her chest, and told him, "You can feel the implant and see I have a life-saving ICD in my chest."

Bob explained that Senator Kennedy asked what he had hoped he would, "Has it gone off?"

Connie replied, "Yes, sir, it has gone off twice. I am still here enjoying my husband, children, and my grandchildren. But, we had to remortgage our house to get this device and allow it to save me."

After that exchange, the senator came back, sat back down in front of me, put his head down, then looked up at me; our eyes met briefly, and then he thanked everyone for coming in and speaking to him about these critical matters.

The senator's secretary escorted the group to the exit door. Then she grabbed Bob's arm and whispered, "Mr. Schriever, you will get this, too!"

After they walked back to meet the rest of the group, Connie shared with Bob, "We had been in Senator Kennedy's office for over forty minutes!"

Bob continued, "Two weeks later, at 9:15 AM, my phone rang. It was Senator Kennedy's secretary. She said, "I called to inform you that on January 1, 2005, Medicare will cover the costs of implanted heart devices such as ICDs and Pacemakers for all senior citizens."

More recently, in 2019, Bob's friend, Bill Pierce, had a hospital bill for his ICD replacement. It came to $100,501.43, all covered by Medicare.

I am personally grateful to Bob Schriever and his dedication to the vital work of the Sudden Cardiac Arrest Association (SCAA). Bob is a true "Heart Champion." My mother's current husband has a Pacemaker and ICD combo unit, and without it, my loving stepfather, "Buzz" Patterson, would not be with us today. I am grateful for

Bob's efforts, past, present and future, and for allowing me to share this much of his story.

Bob continues to work tirelessly in his region to educate high-school students. Bob's Sudden Cardiac Arrest Association (SCAA) New England Chapter trained more than 25,000 students, teachers, and coaches in several areas this past school year. The SCAA New England Chapter has training programs in hands-only CPR, dangers of health challenges like smoking, vaping, and energy drinks. These are the warning signs and symptoms of Sudden Cardiac Arrest (SCA), and hidden heart disease. As an ABF Trained Team, the SCAA New England Chapter is currently working with school districts and medical professionals to incorporate heart-screenings into their program(s).

CHAPTER EIGHT

Anthony said, "I think you should let him go!"

Have you ever had a bad report card from school? Many of us have, and many would have liked to keep the experience to ourselves. Well, Anthony was no different. He must have been nine or ten when he received his first lousy report card. There was no child/parent or teacher/parent meeting about his failing status before accepting the mailed report card. As the person to pick up the mail, I was the first to uncover the news. That night, I gave Allen, Anthony's adoptive dad, an update over our dinner together. Anthony sat stoically in his chair, not moving or saying anything. Between bites, Allen and I discussed forms of punishment appropriate for his "crime" of failing grades, which also included misbehaving in class.

Allen: "Maybe we should ground him from television for a few months?"

Sharon: "No, it might be better to take away his privilege to be on the soccer team."

Allen: "Why not take away the video games and all access to the video arcade?"

Our conversation went back and forth for several minutes, as if Anthony was not even at the table. Then there was a pause in our parental discussion. In a small voice, that sounded very similar to Pee-Wee Herman from the movie, *Pee Wee's Big Adventure*, Anthony whispered, "I think you should let him go!"

Shocked by the plea, Allen and I burst out laughing. We all laughed for an extended amount of time! Anthony's punishment was less severe than any discussed disciplines. He seemed to have dodged that bullet through love and laughter.

Many years later, in Phoenix, Arizona, on Anthony's twenty-first birthday, we hosted a "Celebration of Life" service at Mountain Park Community Church. I shared this story with the people who gathered to honor Anthony. With an emotional plea, I wasn't sure how I could ever muster the courage to "let him go," but the reality of his death was still brutal and gut-wrenching to the core. No mother should have to face these emotional challenges of "letting go of her child," let alone her only child. I still struggle with this anguish daily, more than twenty years later!

It may seem like I have not been able to let him go. I work to advance the mission of the Anthony Bates Foundation. I support organizations that advocate for heart health for children and families. However, what I don't do is wallow in self-pity and sadness. There are still triggers, sad days, and low-energy days, too. I suspect there will be times like these throughout the rest of my life. Anthony's life was short, and I accept that now. I am grateful that he was my son, and I was his mother. Life's lessons have made me grow and become a more loving person that I am today.

CHAPTER NINE

How Anthony picked his dad: Allen Bates

My Dad
By Anthony Bates, age 12, January 7, 1992
English Period 7 - Essay

"I am telling you about my Step-dad. His name is Henry Allen Bates, Jr. He likes to go by Allen Bates. I am going to talk about how I met him, the years I spent together with him, and how I influenced him.

"I met my dad in 1982 in Phoenix, Arizona. I was three-years-old. My Mom (sic) and I were at a launder mat (sic). My Mom (sic) was folding clothes while I was wandering around. Allen was sitting on a chair. He had some candy and a can of soda in his hands. He was a stranger to me. I went up to him and knowing what he had in his hands; I asked him if I could have some candy. He replied, "I'll give you some if you go get your mom." I went, and I got my Mom (sic) to come over where he was sitting. They met each other and talked. They played a game of Ms. Pac Man. A few days later, they went on a date. Three years later, they got married in Wichita, Kansas.

"I influenced my dad a lot because while my mom and dad were dating, he would see me a lot. When they would go on outings together, such as camping, dinner, amusement parks, and other places, I would go, too. Pretty soon, I got so used to him around I would call him dad. We all lived together, a three-person family. Then we moved to Wichita, Kansas, in 1985. They got married that next July.

"A year later, I got adopted by Allen. I always think of him as my real dad because my real dad got a divorce with my mom when I was one year old. I also think of him as my real dad because I never see my real dad. My last name used to be Foote, but since 1986, it has been Bates. I got to know a lot of my dad's friends and relatives, who are my relatives now.

"That is how I met him, the years I spent together with him, and how I influenced my dad. That is also how he influenced me. I am so glad I met him in that launder mat (sic)."

CHAPTER TEN

Anthony's Birth

When I found out I was pregnant, I was seventeen-years-old. I left the doctor's office that day and sat in my car for what seemed to be an hour. I prayed about the baby in my belly. I was excited, happy, afraid, and full of emotion. Maybe it was the flush of hormones, but I knew I would keep my baby, no matter what happened. The message I got back from my prayers was that my child would be my friend. The friend I never had growing up. I thought things would be okay, and I knew we would make it in the world.

I shared my "little gift" with my boyfriend, Joe, soon to be my husband. He seemed as happy as I was. We were okay about starting a family together as a young couple. Thankfully, things were progressing in his job, and we were able to pay our bills and get groceries. What more could we need? He was an Assistant Manager at a Bob's Big Boy. Things were looking good. We were on our way to creating a great family. I realized we were naïve, as young people often are while living an inexperienced, myopic life.

Then the news spread to my family. My sisters were happy to become aunties. Before I got pregnant, I had dropped out of high school to concentrate on working. My sisters were still in school.

After I realized I would become a mother, I could focus on starting my own family.

When I shared the news with my sisters, my mother was at work. I was not brave enough to stay at their house to tell my mother. I had a feeling she wouldn't take the news very well. I shared the news with my sisters and then left. She was still married to our pedophile stepfather and seemingly unfazed that I had moved in with my boyfriend. When she heard the news about me being pregnant, she became hostile and irate. My sisters told me afterward that she was livid. She said to them that I should get an abortion. Later she told me the same thing. She ranted that she could throw my boyfriend in jail for statutory rape because I was just seventeen.

I blew off her threats because I knew she wouldn't take a stand for any one of her daughters. Why start now? Besides, I didn't live under her roof, and I didn't have to play by her rules anymore. I just ignored her and didn't respond to her calls or attempts to discuss MY future.

Before too long, my boyfriend's promotion led us to Flagstaff. We both got jobs up there and got away from my mother's taunts and accusations. I was also working at Bob's Big Boy, as a server, until my pregnancy progressed, so I became a hostess. Being on my feet was tough, but I was young, and the pregnancy seemed so easy. Don't get me wrong; I had a few mishaps during my pregnancy. I cut my thumb on a glass while doing dishes; that incident led to an emergency room visit and three stitches. Then when I was seven months along, I did take a tumble on the last few steps of our two-story condo; that incident led to an extra doctor visit and a cast for my dislocated big toe. Before too long, it was early October, and I was ready to have our baby.

I was a few days past my due date of October 3rd. The doctor was saying that the baby hadn't dropped, and I could go another couple of weeks. By that time, I just wanted the baby out of me. I hadn't seen my feet for months. My belly was so big, I was so uncomfortable I couldn't sleep, and I waddled when I walked.

After the doctor's appointment, I decided to get some air, and I went for a long walk. The fall weather in Northern Arizona was warm, and the sun was bright. There was a light breeze; the leaves rustled in the trees to distract me from the walk's length. I took our new dog with me from our condominium to the restaurant where my boyfriend was working. Not realizing the walking distance, I must have walked a good three miles or more. I had to share the news with my boyfriend that it could be a few more weeks before the baby was born. Of course, I could have called, but it was the busy lunch hour. Once I arrived, the rush was over, and I could sit for a few minutes to share the news. I enjoyed a treat of a yummy gooey hot-fudge cake and then journeyed back to the condominium. That night at 3 a.m., I went into labor.

At first, I didn't believe what was happening considering the news from the doctor. We had prepared for the expectations of labor and delivery. We had previously taken the birthing classes. Besides, we were ready to go to the hospital, as my bag was packed. I woke my boyfriend up at 4 a.m. and said, "We need to go to the hospital. My contractions were about six minutes apart."

Off we went and made our way to the Flagstaff Hospital. Right away, the hospital attendant whisked us up to the labor and delivery floor. My contractions were getting stronger and closer together. How could I do this? I was still a little girl – seventeen-years-old. Would I be a good mother? Would I be blind to my child's needs? On the other hand, would I be a better person because of what I had experienced? Well, there was no turning back!

The doctor came in to tell me it was time to deliver. Yikes! "I think I need a spinal block." The doctor replied, "Too late for that. Your baby is coming now!" As I said, there was no turning back!

All "gowned-up" in surgical attire, my boyfriend, Joe, was right there with me. He coached me along. At times, the pain was excruciating, and I wasn't pleasant to the nurses. I believe many mothers can relate to my anguish. The pain was a "ten," and I felt like I was chewing nails.

Fortunately, the baby came into the world fast! Our baby boy was born at 8:46 a.m. on October 6, 1979. Quite a quick delivery, considering I was so young. It must have been that six-mile walk!

We had already selected names before the baby was born. Amanda, if the baby was a girl or Anthony if the baby was a boy.

As soon as Anthony was born, he was red and crying loudly. The doctor cut his cord, and the nurse cleaned him up a bit. Then they placed him on my chest. He instantly stopped crying. His eyes were wide open, and he gazed into my own crying eyes. We connected at a soul level to a depth that I had never connected with any other being in such a profound way. My heartstrings were singing, and my eyes kept leaking. Through all the doubts and drama, our connection made our bond so real. All of life's challenges washed away at that moment. Our soul-connection showed me that Anthony and I were to share valuable time on earth. Right then, it seemed like he chose me to be his mother!

The nurses took him away to do their assessments and clean him up further. They weighed him, and to my dismay, he was a nine-pound, six-and-a-half ounce baby. Oh my, he was already a big boy! Then, I needed some doctor's attention. My placenta was not coming out. I didn't know why the doctor was worried, but I could have bled to death. She reached inside of me, which brought me out of my euphoria and pulled from my uterus the lethargic placenta. I screamed, "Hey, I'm not an elephant!"

There was some laughter, and relief as she examined the placenta to be sure it was intact. Phew, what an experience! After they cleaned me up, with their help, I went back to my room. Right away, the nurse brought Anthony in to stay with me. From the start, he was a hungry little person. We did breast-feeding. As a new mommy, it was a struggle at first, but we got the hang of it.

Hospitals were beginning to send a new mom and baby home in twenty-four hours or less. After one sleepless night in the hospital, we were discharged before noon the next day and sent home to be a new family. Anthony was born on a weekend, which meant we didn't get the hospital pictures that many new families cherish. But we did take many photos because we were new parents. He was our world.

A few months later, it was Christmas time, and we could get several days off from work. My boyfriend and I wanted to go to Las Vegas from Flagstaff to be married. There was still family drama. I was under eighteen years old and not legal to get married, not even in Nevada. My mother wasn't going to give us the required written note to get married. Nevertheless, somehow she did finally give in and wrote the letter.

On Christmas Eve, we drove to Las Vegas, Nevada, to get married in a little chapel, and then I drove back to Flagstaff while my new husband slept in the car with our baby and his sister, Patty. Patty came to live with us after being a teenage run-away. Our wedding was certainly not romantic, especially having to deal with Patty's "situation." Even then, I didn't feel like our new marriage was a relationship that would last. Why did I do it? I am sure that the tax write-off of a new child and a married couple weighed into our decision. Our relationship seemed so superficial and contractual. It was not a very good reason to get married, but we did it anyway. Growing up is hard to do, at age seventeen, with the burden of a newborn and a husband.

Three months after Anthony's birth, we moved again for jobs at Bob's Big Boy in Kingman, Arizona. Patty went back to Phoenix to live with her mother and stepfather. Joe and I moved to Kingman to live with another manager and his wife. That experience wasn't healthy for a newly married couple with a young baby. It turned out that the people we lived with had trouble conceiving a child, and their jealousy contributed to an unpleasant atmosphere.

The house we shared was extremely cluttered. Even though we had a room to ourselves, there wasn't enough space for a new family to flourish. Most of our furnishings were in storage. We had no privacy or the ability to develop our relationship. In that house, there was lots of screaming, fighting, and more tears. There were too many dogs. I was not happy. Anthony and I needed a safe, stable environment in which to live. Two months into that living arrangement, I called my mother to come to Kingman and get Anthony and me. I was desperate to go back to Phoenix even though it was to my mother and stepfather's house. The living arrangements were temporary. I just needed to get a job and a new place to live. Within two weeks, I had both.

CHAPTER ELEVEN

Return of the Phoenix

Anthony and I moved back to Phoenix. I was eighteen years old and, once again, living in my mother and stepfather's home, which didn't last long. I got a waitressing job and found a group of people to share a house. I moved out of my parents' home and filed for divorce from Joe.

Anthony and I lived in a house with nine other adults and nine children. It was cramped, chaotic, and most of the adults worked at the same restaurant. The rent was cheap, and the new family arrangements were fun, at first. There were fun parties, too. It was great to be single and have my whole life in front of me. However, my desire for a better life for Anthony and me was always the top priority.

The divorce from Joe was final in November 1980. I was married less than a year. I felt like a failure, but a stable environment was a priority. Living on a server's income, as a single mother and a high school dropout, I needed to find a better life for my son and me. It was still the era of newspapers, before the internet. I hunted for jobs in the newspaper. It seemed that medical jobs and computer jobs filled up the most columns in the wanted sections.

When I was in school in Canada, I thought I wanted to be a doctor. When we moved to the States, and we had a big problem getting my Canadian school transcripts sent to my new high school in the States. Looking back in Canada, I remembered a field trip to Simon Frasier University. I had a vivid experience visiting a computer room with all the tape decks spinning in the computer racks or towers. I was in awe of that experience. Maybe I could take some computer classes, I thought.

One of the first jobs I took outside of the food-service industry was in the accounting field. There was an Accounts Payable position open at an assisted-living home in Central Phoenix. I knew how to pay bills, so I must be qualified to be an Accounts Payable clerk. I accepted the job, and my desk was in an office in the non-ambulatory part of the nursing home. The conditions were not pleasant, which helped me realize the sad state of affairs for our elderly. Shortly after starting my accounting job, my supervisor transferred me to the ambulatory building next door. That was a more pleasant work environment.

Assisted-living programs are near and dear to my heart. While working there, I met Carol and Keith Massey. We exchanged pleasantries during their regular visit while looking in on their elderly relatives, Uncle Howard and Aunt Helen. Keith was a friendly man from Oklahoma, and he could start up a conversation with almost anyone. Carol was a professional in the accounting world herself. They took a liking to me, and Anthony, too. Soon after our budding friendship, I began working for Carol at the CPA firm, Acosta, Cordova, and Pittman. For more than a year, I worked in accounting and was their back-up computer operator.

With Carol's encouragement, I completed my GED and enrolled in classes at Phoenix College. I took an introduction-to-computers class and saw the light at the end of my tunnel of despair. Nevertheless, life has a way of giving you twists and turns. There are times where things didn't work out the way I mapped them out in my plan.

There was my traumatic childhood, then my challenging teen years, and finally, in my 20's, I had a new direction. Well, life turned on another dime when I happened to fall in love again, this time with Anthony's help, after a chance meeting of Allen Bates in a Laundromat.

Anthony and Mom '82

After we moved in with my future husband, Allen, it seemed our life was on the right track. We laughed a lot, and he loved my son and me. Individually, we both had personal issues to work through, though. I still hadn't dealt with my abusive childhood. Anthony was sensitive to my emotional traumas and was trying to protect his mommy, even at three years old. Allen had a past marriage that failed and had a manipulative ex-wife. She limited Allen's visitation of their young son, Chris. Over the years, Chris and Allen had many emotional challenges. Her second husband adopted Chris. Chris' life was complicated, too.

Mostly, Allen was patient and supportive. We each had our parent issues to heal. Over time, we decided to move once again. Allen and I disagreed on our moving destination. I wanted to go to Denver with my current employer, a travel agency. He had a job promotion that would allow him to move to Kansas to be closer to his family. We both went our separate ways. After a two-day drive, Anthony and I lived with a friend from my job in Denver. The following Monday, I went to report to work, but I learned the job situation was not at all as advertised. Allen had already moved to Kansas. I called him, and he invited Anthony and me to come to live with him.

In a short time, we all ended up in Kansas. Kansas was the place of Allen's birth. Most of his family lived in Wichita, including his mother, Eve; father, Henry; two sisters, Jan and Terry, and their families. There were many good times and connections to his friends that I hadn't had in my own life. For example, the most extended time that I had a good friend was just a few years, but Allen had friends going back to grade school. His family and friendships were deep connections for Allen in Kansas.

However, Allen was also a broken person. He had a splintered relationship with his father, and his parents experienced grandparent separation from Allen's son, Chris. This family was not a "fairy-tale" family. There were experiences of manipulation, distrust, and pain, many of the things I experienced in my own family. Allen and I bonded because of that pain. Through that pain, we individually felt we both needed healing.

In the five years we were in Kansas, I went to counseling to find answers about my childhood. The depth of my feelings of emotional abandonment by my mother was so strong that I couldn't shake the despair. On top of the sadness, I also experienced physical pain, migraines, stomach, and back pain that followed me through counseling. In my counseling sessions, it became clear that counselors are only there to help you become aware of the depth of your pain. Counseling sessions are not always the place we find true healing. Healing comes with awareness, acceptance, tolerance, and forgiveness.

We also found a small church, the Linwood Park Church, that met in a Wichita park near our house. By that time, Allen and I were married, and Anthony was about eight years old. We started attending church services every weekend. Honestly, I felt that an angel touched my soul at those joyous church services. My heart opened, and the tears flowed, washing away much of the pain I held onto from my childhood. I remember during one of the church services, Anthony asked me why I cried when I prayed. I'm not sure I gave him much of an answer. I didn't understand what was happening to me at the time. I had no idea the gift that was given to me in those healing prayers until years later.

After one of the evening prayer circles I attended, I was speaking to my pastor about life. Allen and I were trying to have more children. The IVF process was expensive and wasn't working. I shared with my pastor that during the prayer circle, I had a vision that my life would be big, "really big!" The image I saw in my mind's eye during my prayer time was an overhead view of the world. It seemed like I was swirling around the earth at light speed. There were contrails following me as I was swirling around faster and faster, around the globe with my hands wide open. Years later, after Anthony died, I reconnected with that pastor, and he reminded me of our talk that night. Looking back now, I would have to agree; my life has been significant! My life has been tragic yet also significant.

Shortly after Allen and I were married, the idea of Anthony's adoption came up. Allen's ex-wife took Allen's biological son out of state, and had his surname changed. To solidify our new family, Allen and I offered to change Anthony's name to Bates. Mind you, Anthony was an old-soul. We figured that out early, based on the many lessons he taught us as a family. So, we posed the idea to him, would you like to be a "Bates," too?

"Yes, of course!" Anthony said. But, we didn't realize there was still a lingering concern in his heart. It wasn't until we got closer to the court date that the discussion of his mixed feelings came out. There was the challenge he felt from the love he had in his heart for his biological father. Mind you; we had lost touch with Joe just a year after our divorce. Anthony and I talked through the issues. As I shared with Anthony, "There is enough love in your heart to love EVERYONE, including your biological father; your new dad, Allen; me; and every-one in our family." He accepted my answer, and that seemed to ease his anxious heart and mind.

We went through the court date with a little surprise for me. Allen and Anthony had discussed his full name. At the time of adoption, a child can change any part of his name. Anthony wanted to take "Allen" as his middle name. Through the adoption, Anthony Allen Bates was reborn to the world.

Anthony Allen Bates

CHAPTER TWELVE

A New Career

It was 1986, and life was moving along in Kansas. Anthony was doing well in school, and Allen was doing well at Safelite Auto Glass. However, I was hungry for more opportunities to build a better lifestyle. Before Kansas, my education was on the back burner, and by then, I happened to be working in another accounting office, this time at Friends University. There were classes I could take to increase my computer skills and allow me to get a leg-up on a career I desired.

However, standing up for myself, as I had learned to do, presented a new challenge. As an accounts-payable clerk, I felt there were some deficiencies in the process of the payables in my job duties. I took my ideas to the department supervisor. He immediately shot down my suggestions and barked at me, "You should keep your ideas to yourself and go back to clerk school." That didn't sit well with me at all. I took my ideas about my job functions and my concerns about my supervisor to the department head. Suffice it to say; I was transferred into the computer room by the end of the month.

Almost immediately, I came across an opportunity that would change my life. I enrolled in the Report Program Generator (RPG) programming classes that I would need to understand the language of the IBM System thirty-six we had in the computer room. RPG is a high-level programming language for business applications. At first, the computer language was hard, exciting, and challenging all at the same time. The computer language structure was intricate and magical, almost like reading notes on sheet-music pages. During my school years in Canada, I had three years of playing the clarinet and one flute year. I also studied French for several years, which gave me the advantage of learning a computer language. As my skills progressed, I could almost do the coding in my head with my eyes closed. I was having fun experiencing the computer responses to my commands, just like an orchestra's maestro.

Through years at the university, I made friends with good people. Two students, Karen Kinser, Susan Lucas, and I spent lots of time together after work. Karen was a leader in school and encouraged my new educational pursuit. We also commiserated about the struggles we shared in our early family life but found ways to laugh off life's challenges. I am grateful we stayed in touch for many years. However, I became sad that we lost contact a few years after Anthony passed away. Too many email changes put us out of reach.

However, during my time in my new position, that former supervisor that I had in Accounting was still at the university. The computer room wasn't far from the Accounting Department. Almost daily, I would see him in the halls. There was real tension in the air, and I didn't like being put down or chastised for expressing ideas to help the company. After only one year in the computer room, I started looking around at other opportunities in the computer language I had just learned. Soon after my search began, I found a new job at an insurance company in Goddard, Kansas, not far from Wichita.

The insurance company owner had a son-in-law who was breeding exotic animals on the property and brokering them to zoos. There were lemurs, antelope, birds, snow leopards, giraffe, and more. Nevertheless, most of all, my favorite animals were the tigers. Their white tigers were very magical to me. Every day I would go to work and see the animals in the fields and distant cages. It was almost surreal. I worked there for two years and loved the experience and atmosphere.

CHAPTER THIRTEEN

Fishing and Scouts with Anthony!

The work I had in the insurance company's computer room was fun and challenging. I was learning a lot about the multiple levels of programming. Some things were comfortable, and some things didn't come to me as quickly as I had hoped. There were new things to learn every time a new computer upgrade occurred. I was enjoying the process and challenges that were in front of me. The data was speaking to me subliminally as well. There were times I would have a problem in the computer program, and seeing the answer wasn't coming very quickly, I would sleep on it. The next morning, the answers would appear. Just like magic -- or was it divine inspiration?

The animals in the fields were enchanting. On occasion, we were allowed supervised visits to them. I was in awe of the magical power the animals had over me, especially the tigers. There was a white tiger breeding pair; the father was orange with a recessive white gene; the mother was white with blue eyes. The animal keepers fed the tigers a whole frozen chicken every day but Sundays, claiming the hunger kept them wild. While in Kansas, this experience heightened my appreciation for wild animals.

One spring, while I was at that computer job, the female tiger had three cubs. The animal keepers took the cubs from the mother at three-days-old, to be hand raised. For better domestication, the office staff was allowed to interact, hold, and feed the wild cubs. I was able to hold and feed one of the baby tigers. Even at a young age, the power of that animal was overwhelming. The experience was sad and energizing at the same time. Tears rolled down my cheeks, and my heart broke, knowing the tiger cubs would remain caged even as adult big-cats. The Kansas breeding program allowed other zoos in the nation to have a white tiger for such a breeding opportunity.

The grounds of the insurance company also had a fishpond. The pond was quite significant to the property and overstocked with fish. The owners encouraged employees and their families to fish in the pond to help reduce the fish population. One of the things I was able to do for Anthony was to teach him to fish.

Some of my good memories of my childhood were with our family fishing expeditions. When I was a small girl, my mother and stepfather would bring the family camping to the interior of British Columbia to a location referred to as the "one-hundred-mile house." During those trips, we would be far from the city life we lived in during the school year. Then we would camp for two weeks in the woods by a lake. There were loons, rainbow trout a-plenty, and bald eagles, too. We learned a lot about camping, fishing, and living off the land. We had fish for lunch, dinner, and sometimes breakfast. We were so sick of fish after two weeks. Nevertheless, those memories were the fun ones from my childhood. That was years before the abuse started.

After I married Allen, we took Anthony to our first family fishing and camping trip at Winfield Lake outside Wichita, where I taught him what I knew about fishing. Allen tried to teach him, but successful fishing is about placing the worm correctly or selecting the right bait for the fish to bite.

While I did campsite chores, Allen and Anthony went fishing for the first hour. When they caught nothing, I jumped in to share my learned-skill of "worm on a hook." As soon as the worm was in the water, there were bites and fish took the hook. That got everyone excited about camping and fishing, especially me. We would borrow Allen's parents' camper, so we didn't have to sleep in tents. It was a little more enjoyable than the tent experiences I had in Canada.

With the fun, we had fishing, Anthony, age ten by then, brought his pole and a friend to my insurance company's computer office one morning to fish all day. I worked in the office, and Anthony, with his fishing-buddy, dipped their poles in  the pond throughout the day. This time they were fishing for catfish, which were quite plentiful in the pond. By the time I was ready to go home, they had a big fish string that day.

I was in my car, waiting for the boys and I heard loud, boisterous screams. I ran over to the pond, and Anthony had just pulled in a huge catfish. That fish was almost ten pounds and the biggest catfish he had ever landed. There continued to be excitement and celebration all night long. I think that fish grew in size after it got out of the pond, too. Well, that is the story I tell!

Anthony had joined the Cub Scouts in Kansas. He was a Webelo Cub Scout. Those first few years that Anthony was in scouting, I was his Den Leader, helping him grow and mature into the young man he was becoming. There were fishing outings and contests in Scouts that Anthony entered. Every time he won, I would pat myself on the back for teaching him how to fish.

While in Kansas, Anthony also started participating in sports. He tried soccer … "too much running," he would say. He loved base-ball and enjoyed catching and pitching, too. However, his real love was football. There was a league in Kansas called the "Beech" league sponsored by Beech Aircraft. He played two seasons in Kansas and excelled in the running-back position. His little cousins, Hilary and Katrina, were cheerleaders for his team. Therefore, when we went to Anthony's games, the whole Wichita area, Bates Family, would be there.

The second year Anthony played Beech League Youth Football; I helped as a defensive coach. It wasn't that I knew a lot about the game; I just wanted to be there for my son. I tried to understand his excitement for the sport and talk to him about plays and experiences. Later in college, while in the stands, I would remark about plays and penalties, and my seatmates were surprised I knew so much about the game.

CHAPTER FOURTEEN

Back to Arizona – A Much Better Decision!

The winter of 1989 was brutal in Kansas. The wind chill was fifty-seven below zero. I was a very young girl from St. Paul, Minnesota. I don't remember much about the winters because I was just four or five when my mother divorced my father and moved our family back to her home city, Vancouver, Canada. Even winters in Canada were not in the extreme category compared to Kansas. I had not experienced a frigid winter like that in my life. Allen's job was going nowhere, so he looked into transferring back to Arizona. By 1990, we were ready to head back to the "Valley of the Sun" and excited about the prospects before us.

We moved back to Phoenix in the spring of 1990. My career was sound, and I had a new job within two weeks. We found a lovely rental house close to the same area where I grew up in Phoenix, not far from my mom's house. Also, two of my three sisters, Teresa and Diane, still lived in Phoenix.

We signed Anthony up for Little League in the spring when we arrived in Phoenix. He excelled on the team and was a star player. He had a high batting average, hit many home runs, and enjoyed playing catcher and pitcher. After his first season was over, we found out he wouldn't be eligible for the playoff team because we lived outside the league boundaries. What a shock for Anthony and us, as parents, trying to give him a good baseball experience. I didn't realize how much politics goes into youth sports until that very moment. There were other lessons of "sports politics" later on after Anthony got into high school.

By the time fall rolled around that first year back in Arizona, Pop Warner youth football league had weight and age restrictions to our dismay. Anthony was eleven soon to be twelve years old, and the weight class for him was 130 pounds. Benched the first year, Anthony was already over 150 pounds. He had always been a husky "big boy" throughout his life. Crushed from the lack of participating in his favorite sport, Anthony had to sit out that football season. I told him I would help him with an exercise program and a healthier diet, too.

Several mornings each week, we would jog on the canal behind our house. We also had a home gym that Anthony started using regularly. He cut his food portions and watched what he ate for the whole year. He was making great strides in a healthy lifestyle.

In the meantime, he played soccer and baseball the next spring. He still kept his grades up and did well in his classes. Anthony had some minor struggles during school because he would "act out" from boredom in these low-level courses. Mostly, he would become too social. His report card noted, "Too much talking" in a few of his classes, and Anthony would receive consequences for his actions, as we felt that was good parenting. A lousy report during grading periods would mean he would have privileges taken away. As an example, video games were not allowed during those times.

By the time the next football season rolled around, Allen and I had purchased our first house in Awhatukee. It was still in Phoenix, but south of South Mountain, just west of Tempe. The area had been expanding to new family homes, previously set up as a retirement community. The schools were fresh, and the city was bubbling with new families. We enrolled Anthony in his new school, Kyrene Akimel A-al Middle School, and he had new sports teams to contend with in our new community.

That is when we found a new level of politics in youth sports. There were "travel leagues" and "after-season leagues" that helped the players (baseball mainly) get a leg up on the competitive field of youth sports. Anthony excelled on his Little League Baseball teams, but without a spot on a "travel league" team, it was too late to help him get on the high-school baseball team. When he got to high school, the coaches had already decided which players would make up their teams.

By that time, Anthony was trim enough to get back on the Pop Warner ranks. He played for two years in Pop Warner football and had great seasons leading up to his high-school football career.

Life seemed to be going well. Anthony was in sports and doing well in school. My computer career had excelled when we moved back to Arizona. Jobs were plentiful, and I hopped around a few different employers trying to find an excellent workplace. However, Allen struggled to find success in his work life. Safelite laid-off Allen, and the jobs he qualified for in the "blue-collar" workforce were hard to find. Four-thousand people were vying for the same warehouse jobs he would apply for, and the rejection was painful.

For two years, Allen was without steady work. I was going to school at the University of Phoenix, attempting to finish my degree. Anthony was in scouts, working on his Eagle Scout Project, trying to finish before high school consumed him. He was fifteen years old when he completed his Eagle Scout Project and got his award. Allen was still struggling, and our marriage was crumbling.

The tipping point came when Allen and Anthony had a physical altercation. Allen and I seemed to work through the increased bickering between us, but his fight with Anthony was my last straw. I kicked Allen out. At that point, I was making enough salary to pay for the house and family needs in my career. Allen needed to get his life together. I was frustrated with our marriage and needed him out of mine.

Nevertheless, Allen and I agreed not to let Anthony manipulate us as parents. We recognized the importance of co-parenting. We needed to make our decisions together for Anthony's best interest and for our own sanity.

Overall, Allen was a good father to Anthony. Even though I loved Allen, he needed to find his way. I felt that my successes were weighing him down. I'm not sure if that is true, because we never talked about it to each other. It was kind of a feeling I had at the end of our marriage.

By the time Allen and I divorced, I was a contract-computer programmer. That allowed me to stay out of the office politics I found so disheartening as a female in a man's world, particularly in Information Technology (IT.) There were times of struggle in my career, experiencing sexual harassment, being over-looked by the bosses for raises and promotions, or overlooked for challenging projects. I just had to persevere through those issues to allow my career to grow.

In my third decade of life, I was closing in on my bachelor's degree in Management and Marketing. I was single, enjoying my career, and my son was doing very well in school. Then I experienced a disheartening event that ended my joy in the higher learning experience. I got to the end of my course work early in my stint at the University of Phoenix (UOP). When I had enrolled in the course work, the Admissions Counselor advised me that I could "test out" of the computer courses. My current career was in computers, which allowed me real-world experience and knowledge in those courses. UOP even provided me with experiential credit for my computer career work. As I neared graduation, the Exit Counselor at UOP told me I would have to take their computer course that cost more than $600 to complete. I was ready to graduate with my class and anxious to get my degree. The exit counselor told me the first counselor was wrong about being able to "test out" of the computer courses. To this day, I still feel that they changed the rules and never bothered to tell me until just before graduation. I experienced more politics and more disappointment! Either way, I was disappointed in the higher-education political arena.

I walked in my gown at the UOP commencement, but I never completed the course work. The bureaucracy of "for-profit" learning and higher education politics extinguished my hope for a degree.

Now amid the COVID-19 pandemic, with no screening events taking place, I looked into some educational options during this downtime.

ABF won't be back in schools right away after the lifted "stay at home" orders. The questions I face at this stage in my life, five decades of living, should I go back to school? Why not, life is a learning experience and big classroom. I made a new choice to pursue a career in Cardiac Ultrasound. My journey to help people continues.

In high school, Anthony was on the varsity squad at Mountain Pointe High School. He was doing well on the football field and quite vocal about me not finishing my course work at the University of Phoenix to receive a degree. He teased me that he would get his college degree before I did. As it turns out, that was true. Even though he received his degree posthumously, I still don't have my "piece of paper." I just have the one (or two) from the "School of Hard Knocks" in my hip pocket.

Sometimes, I wish I would have gone back to complete my degree or maybe get one in Non-profit Management. For the ABF database advancement, becoming a certified ultrasound technician would bring more credibility to ABF. However, "driving the bus," washing the floors, and administering the heart tests are not good business practices for a CEO. Previous desires took a back seat to the current state of affairs. I am proud of the work accomplished by ABF. As well, I am proud of my life accomplishments. The lives we have saved and the people we have influenced are much more valuable to me than any paper or certificate of credible skills.

Anthony's first high school year in football was shortened by a broken forearm; however, he continued on the football team through high school. Those years were a lot of fun for me. I got involved in the Mountain Pointe High School Football Booster Club. It was reminiscent of my volunteer years in Anthony's grade school. In those days, I was a PTA President in Kansas as well as his Scout Den Leader and eventually became the Football Booster President in Arizona. As in PTA and Scouting, the same six parents show up to do all the work; at minimum, attend the planning meetings. Football booster parents were required to work several shifts in the concession stands during their son's football season. That was true for freshman, junior varsity, and varsity squads. Rounding up the "volunteers" was much more helpful, as the coaches' encouragement came from the players to the parents. For the most part, everyone got involved. That process also taught me the importance of "top-down" required involvement. If a parent didn't show up, the football player didn't start the next game.

The varsity-squad parents were the most active. Each varsity parent still had hopes and aspirations for their son to play sports in college. Many of the football players also played other sports. While I was in the booster organization, we created an "advertisement program" for the varsity games. Selling advertisements to local businesses turned out to be a great way to make money for the team.

In 1994, Mountain Pointe High School (MPHS) was the Tempe Union High School District's newest school. Anthony's class was the first full class for the new school. That meant MPHS would have a four-year graduating senior level for the first time. Parent involvement filled the booster and high school process with the community, full of excitement, fun, and energy. Friday nights would bring the community together and fill the stands as we watched our young men reach adulthood.

Coach Karl Kiefer was at the helm. He had a long history in Arizona football and started his career as a young local football player at Arizona State University (ASU.) When he began coaching high school football, his wins began to exceed his losses, and people noticed. Also, Coach Kiefer shared his spiritual faith with the boys. He encouraged the players to be involved in the Fellowship of Christian Athletes (FCA). Before the beginning of each football season, the players had to sign a contract of expected behavior, school requirements, and team discipline. The structure and commitment Coach Kiefer had to assist these young men into adults was heartfelt. Not all the players were happy about the program, but Anthony never complained.

Some players dropped out or washed out. However, Anthony and his good friend, Gary Ensminger, and other young men, flourished in the MPHS football program and life lessons offered by Coach Kiefer. That became evident earlier this year when I attended Coach Kiefer's celebration of life ceremony in early 2020. Shared during the service were life experiences many successful men shared with Coach Kiefer and his lessons. Former high school football player, coach, and educator, Dick Baniszewski (Coach Bano), said it well, "Coach

Kiefer made so many men out of so many boys. He was the epitome of integrity and grit." Now Coach is at eternal rest, sharing Heaven with my son and many others who have gone before us.

As the Football Booster Club President, I had the opportunity to speak with Coach Kiefer about their needs and desires. The first year we had the new "programs," the booster club raiser raised more than $20,000. Also, profits from the concession stand helped the MPHS teams. We could reseed the field, get additional equipment for the team, and feed the varsity boys before their big game at a local restaurant. It was extraordinary and fun. I remember one exchange Coach and I had about the team. I commented to him on the players being good boys. He said, "Not all the players are good boys." I am sure he had inside information that he was shielding me from, and honestly, I didn't want to know what he knew. I was just grateful that my son was a good boy.

Before Anthony graduated from high school, my stepfather died. On a fateful day, I pulled Anthony out of school to go to the hospital to support his grandmother, my mother. It was another painful experience for me. Even though my stepfather never asked me for forgiveness, I stood with my head held high, knowing the truth of his abuse I revealed to the family. Don't get me wrong, I did forgive him in my heart for the abuses, and he did provide for my mother. Through all that pain, we did break the cycle of abuse. He never admitted to me he was wrong. His death closed that door.

After Anthony finished his final year in high school football, we thought there would be many college scholarships. Boy, were we wrong. He didn't get any offers from schools in Division I. Nevertheless, by that time, he had his sights on Kansas State University. I wasn't sure why Anthony was looking toward Kansas. I just remember it being so cold.

It turns out that the year we had left Kansas was the first year Head Football Coach Bill Snyder took the helm at Kansas State University. He was taking on the record of the most football losses of all time for the University, attempting a record turn-around that no one thought possible. By the time Anthony graduated high school in 1997, Coach Snyder was making a name for Kansas State University in football. Allen and Anthony watched the rise together. I was not aware of the fandom they had created.

Do you know that only one percent of high school athletes in this country get a college scholarship for sports? With such a high emphasis on sports in this country, that is a phenomenal disparity for many young high school students to face. Student-athletes make sacrifices with hours of training that often impacts on relationships with family and friends. These sacrifices ride on the need to get a scholarship into the right school. Anthony graduated with a 4.67 GPA (out of 4.0) with the gifted program and college-credit level classes added an extra .67 to his GPA. Anthony had been taking accelerated high school classes that allowed extra points in his GPA and college credits. Besides, he was within the seventh percentile of his graduating class of over 700 students. However, he had no real offers to attend a Division 1 athletic program that would allow him to play for the big schools. His prospects were bleak. If he "walked on" at any state college, his Arizona academic scholarship would count against the Arizona school's allotted athletic scholarships. The Arizona state schools University of Arizona, Arizona State University, and Northern Arizona University all turned their backs on Anthony as an athlete even though he had a state academic scholarship.

There seem to be too many rules when it comes to college sports. The academic scholarship rule makes it so difficult for a smart, educated student to be an athlete. How could anyone profess to understand all the rules and regulations? It is sad to see that youngsters with athletic talent and smarts can't even get into the schools within their state.

Anthony and I had a heart-to-heart conversation about his life-long aspirations. He felt he had no other choice but to attend community college to await an offer from a Division 1 university. Anthony was seventeen years old and trying to make a life-impacting decision. Remembering that conversation as if it were yesterday, I heard his feelings of angst and disappointment that filled him with despair for the game he grew to love so very much. Anthony professed, "Mom, I just want to play football!" My eyes welled up as I knew my son was passionate about the sport. I told him right then, "I will help you and do whatever I can to support you in your dreams to play football."

Anthony decided to play ball at the community college level at the local Phoenix College. Anthony worked to improve his skills to make another try for the big schools after his first season with the team. The good news was other teammates of Mountain Pointe High School Pride Lions wanted to continue to play football. Gary Ensminger, Anthony's best friend in high school, and Dennis Gregory were among the high-school teammates that decided to go the same route as Anthony to Phoenix College. Their new coach was John Allen. He was a wonderful, supportive man to Anthony, Gary and the entire team.

The not so good news was that the Phoenix College Bears didn't win many games. How does that look for any player attempting to make it to the "Big Leagues?" The first season Anthony and Gary were at Phoenix College; there was only one "W" on the record books. Each player was hoping to continue their dreams on the next level. Coach Allen helped Anthony and Gary make game tapes and ship them to football programs that interested these young men. In this junior-college experience, only one offer came in for Anthony. Sam Houston University offered Anthony a scholarship after the first year, and he went on his first college trip. He wasn't impressed with the humidity in Houston, Texas or the school. Besides, it wasn't Kansas State University. Anthony felt forced to wait another year. He didn't need the college credits, his grades were fabulous, but he just wanted to play football at a Division I school. He continued to wait for Kansas State University!

During the second football season at Phoenix College, Kansas State University started contacting Anthony. He got very excited! Coach Mo Latimore regularly called, usually on Wednesday nights, to discuss the previous week's game after receiving the most recent tape. Coach knew the time Anthony would return home, but he still called a few minutes early to chat with me. It was a strategic ploy to get to know Anthony's mom and hear another perspective of the young recruit's progress.

Anthony's grades were excellent, and his football skills had improved. He just wanted a shot at a Division I school. He spent more time in the weight room and in the kitchen, too. The grocery bill doubled in size, and his body-mass bulked up. Anthony remained optimistic.

After Anthony's final season at Phoenix College, I made the career decision in early November 1999 to head to the East Coast for a computer contract job related to Y2K. These jobs came with high dollars and significant career opportunities. I traveled to my new gig for two weeks and then came home every other weekend. That gave Anthony more responsibility and less parental pressure to find the right university offer.

There was a lot of activity in the recruiting arena. Anthony went on two more recruiting trips, the first to Brown University and the next to Boston College. He had an offer on the table from the University of New Mexico to accompany his friend from high school, Gary Ensminger. According to the 1998 guidelines of college athletic recruitment, an athlete could only travel four times on recruitment trips. Therefore, Anthony was holding out for his fourth trip for Kansas State University. However, Gary later chose to go to Hastings University in Nebraska. Then after Anthony's trips to Brown University and Boston College, he had a decision to make. He hesitated and contemplated the offers on the table; his dream offer from Kansas State University was not coming.

In 1998, the Kansas State University Football Wildcats ranked second in the nation and finished the regular season undefeated (11-0). The Big Twelve Championship game was against tenth-ranked Texas A&M University, Kansas State lost in double-overtime, losing their chance at a national championship. I watched that game while I was in New Jersey. The next day, I called Coach Latimore and left a voice-mail to share my condolences for the hard-fought loss. Nevertheless, a few days later, Kansas State University Football was selected for the Alamo Bowl game against Purdue University. A few weeks later, however, Kansas State met its second loss in the 1998 Alamo Bowl game.

Between the Big Twelve Championship game and the Alamo Bowl game, Anthony received a phone call from Coach Bill Snyder. At the beginning of the phone call, Anthony shared with Coach Snyder that Coach Mo Latimore had previously stated that Anthony "would not be invited to K-State." Coach Snyder was very gracious and shared with Anthony that "your name is still on my list of calls, so let's talk anyway." For thirty minutes, Anthony answered Coach Snyder's questions about his desire to be on the Kansas State University's football team and his life goals. When Anthony shared with me his conversation with Coach Snyder, I was over the moon with excitement. Anthony was apprehensive because Coach Latimore had been so frank that he would not be getting a K-State offer to play football. I held out hope and said a prayer.

The KSU losses at the end of the 1998 winning season resulted in Head Defensive Coordinator Coach Mike Stoops' departure from KSU to Oklahoma University (OU) to coach with his brother, Head Coach Bob Stoops. This coaching change rippled throughout the KSU team resulting in half the recruits, several players, and other coaches leaving for OU as well! Finally, the football heavens opened up for Anthony. That is when "The trip, the offer, and the chance of a lifetime arrived!"

After Christmas in 1998, Anthony took his long-awaited journey to Manhattan, Kansas. He had to wait until his return to Arizona to commit to Kansas State University, but he was ready to go. Back in Phoenix, Allen was with Anthony when he signed his contract to attend K-State and become a KSU Wildcat forever.

On January 9, 1999, Anthony packed up a U-haul truck and towed his little pickup to his move to Manhattan, Kansas. He was making a life for himself — the life he had always wanted. I was so proud of Anthony for his persistence, perseverance, and for not giving up on his dream. We were all so happy for him.

Living his dream was tremendous but hard; focused but strict; a significant commitment and secluded. There wasn't time for a young, dedicated athlete to have a job or much of social life, either. In this first semester, Anthony excelled in school as well in the weight room. His first spring game was okay, but a redshirt junior-college transfer was not ideal in Coach Snyder's building plan.

After his second spring game in April 2000, Anthony's marked improvement was ready to be second-string behind defensive end leader, Mario Fatafehi. Mario later went on to play in the NFL for the Arizona Cardinals and Denver Broncos, Anthony's two most favorite NFL teams. All Anthony needed to do was complete the summer workouts and improve every day. He never had the opportunity to make the Kansas State University Football team in 2000. He died the last day in July, right after his workout in the KSU weight room.

CHAPTER FIFTEEN

Heavenly Communications with Anthony

After a loved one passes, there is yearning and longing to connect between our separated worlds. Some people have clues of their presence through songs on the radio, signs of fun activities they shared from the past, totem insects or butterflies that spend an extraordinary amount of time lingering among you. There are multitudes of books, articles, and movies documenting such experiences. I had many of my own. The number "91" is significant to me, as that was Anthony's jersey number at Kansas State University, where he played. Also, the number "75" was notable in that it was Anthony's Mountain Pointe High School and Phoenix College football jersey number. However, when your loved one makes an appearance through dream messages, communication seems more probable. At times, my dreams seemed so real. Here are a few examples of my own Anthony connections of life after death:

An angel appears:

In late August 2000, two weeks after arriving back home in Little Ferry, New Jersey from Manhattan, Kansas; I had an enjoyable experience in a dream about my son. During that vivid dream, Anthony escorted me to the billowing clouds in the sky as he demonstrated his agility of the newly fashioned wings. He was making rollercoaster loops in the air circling overhead and around me as I watched in wonder.

"Look at me, mom!" Anthony exclaimed. Many a mother has heard this phrase during their child's youth.

I hesitantly awoke from that dream to look at the clock on the dresser. It read at 2:10 a.m. When I turned back to look at the window at the foot of the bed, larger than life, my son was smiling at me; all dressed in shimmering white. At that moment, Anthony and I spoke no words as a gentle peace flowed through my body. It was a feeling of peace shared between the two angels, one in Heaven and one on Earth.

A gift received:

Several years after Anthony's death, I felt stuck in my despair. Grief does not come with a timetable. We never "get over" the loss of a child. Grief cannot be cured after any number of years. If I believed I could heal, I would! Many people carry grief as a "badge" or a "sentence." We wear the "badge" when we are honoring our child. We take on the "sentence" when we live in the pit of grief, isolated and alone.

Grief can rear its ugly head at various stages and occasions when life continues after losing a loved one. Graduations, weddings, births, and even additional deaths of other loved ones can spark the "ugliness of grief." I couldn't just go on. In these times, I wanted my son back. I was angry at the world for not being more proactive and supportive of the screening programs. I was mad that children seemed to be dying in more significant numbers, and no one seemed to care.

One early morning during my depressed period, I experienced a very long, vivid dream at the playground of Chisholm Elementary schoolyard in Wichita, Kansas. I envisioned Sallie, Anthony's childhood cat, and Sammie, his dog, playing in the schoolyard, though both had died before Anthony's death. The sight of these animals playing together was a bizarre spectacle. I watched them in dismay for what seemed to be several minutes.

On the school property, as in the days when Anthony was a student, several portable classrooms were also staged by the basketball hoops in the back of the main building. During the years he was at Chisholm Elementary, I had been Anthony's Cub Scout Webelo Den Leader. Familiar with the area and the portable classrooms that had housed those meetings, I entered the room with a door ajar. Inside the portable classroom, there was a horseshoe-shaped table layout. A dozen or more people were seated on the outside of the tables. Anthony was sitting at the head of the table, approximately of high school age, yet he seemed more massive than the people sitting around the tables.

"Come sit by me, mom," Anthony said gently.

"Why are Sallie and Sammie outside here playing?" I asked inquisitively.

"They come here with me all the time. Isn't that cute?" Anthony explained.

I shrugged off the answer, found a folded chair against the wall, and carried it over to sit by his side. There were balloons around the room as well as refreshments in the back of the room. It wasn't a birthday gathering, so I was still confused about the type of celebration that had commenced. Then Anthony urged the guests to continue the event. One of the guests came forth and handed Anthony a gift bag. He thanked the young man, seemingly familiar to me, but out of context for the dream location. Anthony pulled the tissue paper out of the bag, and then words came floating out, expressions of gratitude, life events, and praise for Anthony. This process went on with one guest after the next guest for several minutes until everyone had a turn. Then Anthony turned to me.

"What did you bring me, mom?" Anthony inquired. I had heard that question from Anthony on many of my returns from a business trip. I would bring him tchotchkes, T-shirts, snow globes, or items from cities he had never visited. However, this time I was empty-handed.

"I didn't bring you anything. Besides, I'm mad at you!" I remarked.

"Why are you mad at me?" Anthony asked.

"You died!" I exclaimed.

"Oh, mom, get over it!" Anthony pleaded.

I was jolted awake from that dream. My heart was racing, and I was still perplexed and angry. I had many sleepless nights after that experience. Not wanting to get over a loss that was so vast and deep meant I might have to move away from our earthbound connections. "Time heals all wounds," they say, but in the case of a child, my only child, life was never the same after Anthony died. Life just became different.

CHAPTER SIXTEEN

My Faith and Connection to Hurricane Katrina

In 2005, thanks to Hurricane Katrina, things shifted for me. A cardiologist, Dr. Shmuel (Mooly) Shapira, had his practice shut down due to the floods. He had to relocate to New York while he waited for the New Orleans flood to recede. When he returned to his office, his echocardiogram machine was on the second floor, with no water damage. The new practice he had joined already had equipment, so the best thing was to donate the machine.

I was then contacted by Ken Peak, sales-representative, for Siemens Medical Solutions, as he had helped me borrow machines during our events in Arizona and Kansas. He asked me if I would like to receive the echocardiogram machine as a donation. Of course, my answer was an instant, "yes!" ABF was gifted our first ultrasound machine by the generosity of Dr. "Mooly" Shapira and the destruction caused by Hurricane Katrina.

That wasn't the only shift that occurred for me due to Hurricane Katrina. When the storm arose, the event organizers postponed a conference I was going to attend in Louisiana. The meeting was the first U.S. conference to outline the importance of prevention of Sudden Cardiac Arrest (SCA) in athletes, "Mississippi Summit on Sudden Death in Athletes" hosted by the University of Mississippi Medical Center and Dr. John (Jack) Payne. Due to Hurricane Katrina's devastation to Mississippi and Louisiana, the conference organizers decided to reschedule the event to February 2006, which allowed me to attend the Unity of Phoenix Chaplain Program Training.

That conference took place a few months later, in Jackson, Mississippi. The weather on that trip was not cooperating, which caused a change in my already adjusted travel plans. When I arrived in Dallas, the airline had canceled my next flight to Jackson even though Texas's skies were sunny, with no threat of an ice storm. Well, I wasn't going to stand for a little bad weather. I arrived at the rental-car counter to get a car and drive to Jackson. By that time, other travelers had the same idea. I made friends with a few women while in a long line at the counter. "Who is heading to Jackson, Mississippi?" I shouted to the line of people around me. Two women, whose names I don't recall, raised their hands, and we joined forces to drive through the night to the conference.

Leaving Dallas at 5 p.m., the trip would usually take seven or eight hours to drive. As a seasoned long-haul driver, I did all the driving. The three of us women made our way to Jackson, finally arriving at 3 a.m. The ice gave us some trouble when we reached the state border from Texas into Louisiana. Once we hit the bad weather, I had to drive 30 MPH, and sometimes less, for the last few hundred miles. However, the connection with the women in the car made the trip worth the miles. One was a Federal Emergency Management Agency

(FEMA) worker displaced from her home and family in Texas to work the Hurricane Katrina storm damages. The other was a displaced resident of Mississippi and had issues with the process through the storm repairs. I held the healing energy for those women due to my recent chaplain training through the Unity of Phoenix Chaplain Program.

The Unity of Phoenix Chaplain Program Training course requirement is mandatory attendance for the six-week training sessions. One of the sessions fell within the weekend of the original date for the Mississippi Conference. With the conference canceled, God and Hurricane Katrina opened the door for me to be a chaplain. I learned a lot from Reverend Lei Lanni Burt. She was the creator and the head of the chaplain program. She taught people to draw within, drop to your heart, pray together, and support each other through life's journey. We didn't have to fix each other. We just had to support one another. The gift of loving a person through his or her experiences of life was magical.

I went to my first training weekend with my friends, Diane and Wendy, plus many delightful souls. We connected in profound ways and supported each other through the healing of being open to God. One of the most important lessons of being a Unity of Phoenix Chaplain is "family privacy." This rule was valid for my Bates Family and the Kansas State Family and also my Unity of Phoenix Family. The rule states, "Family business is not shared outside the family." The only person who could share the "business" was the person or persons to whom the experience had happened—making the "business" only for those affected. Gossip was forbidden. As in the Unity Chaplain Program, so was it within the Bates Family. In the Chaplain program, when we prayed together, the prayers stayed between God and the people praying. At no time were others privileged to hear the information shared. The only expectation of the rule was when someone's life was in danger; otherwise, everything stayed confidential. There were strict rules to remain in the Unity of Phoenix Chaplain Program and continue as a Chaplain. Attending the training courses and supporting church services was part of those strict rules.

That is a good lesson for everyone, including me. Gossip does not serve the greater good of anyone. Whispers hurt, silence hurts, but sharing someone else's news is no business of the person sharing the news or story. Keep in mind, personal issues will always find a way out, or the people holding onto the problem will work out the problems and issues.

I was in the Unity of Phoenix Chaplain Program as a Unity Chaplain for three years, from 2005 through 2008. My heart was hurting from my childhood trauma, my failed marriages, and loss of my dear son, Anthony. The program gave me healing strength for many of my pains. The program also offered me hope to my life and my life's work, the Anthony Bates Foundation.

As a Unity Chaplain, I found an eight-week grief-counseling program at another church, Community Church of Joy. Not all healing has to occur in one building or with one program. I recommend shopping around the community, researching options and programs that can help you heal your heart's pain and sorrow. Grief comes in many shapes and sizes, just like people. You deserve to find peace and comfort on this earth. I did! Yet, I must continue to focus on retaining my peace, support, and joy with prayer, meditation, and physical activities!

I went to the church program with Jim Jacobus, the brother of Sandy Wilkins my school district work partner. Jim had lost his wife to cancer a few years before. We cried together and healed at depths on many levels. During those sessions, I learned about my jumbled emotions and mixed stages of grief. The stages of grief were attacking my life's essence. The grief emotions resemble a jumbled bowl of spaghetti. After a significant loss, feelings don't come at us in a straight line, one at a time or with a timetable. Over time, I learned to adjust and become gentler with myself. I recognized the times that are hardest to control, and that need more self-care in my life. I hope each person that experiences a profound loss can find healing at a soul level. Be gentle with yourself.

CHAPTER SEVENTEEN

My Grief Journey

With my connections and friendships gained within the Unity of Phoenix Chaplain Program, I made good headway on my issue with the seething anger that rode in my belly. I opened up to regular meditation practice, physical activities, and hikes' in the hills of urban Phoenix.

The loss of a child, for any reason, brings up so many control issues. We are not in control when a child dies, which is a horrendous experience in a mother's life. We have no control over others and no control over many circumstances. However cruel that a child's death may seem, the reality is we have lost not only our child but also our control over almost everything. Sometimes we must let go of the urge to control, and the healing will begin.

By no means am I a grief expert. I am only an expert on my grief journey. Each person who has traveled this path, carrying the sad "cross of grief" has different needs. Some people find ways to cope with their children's death through their work, hobbies, faith, or family. However, grief expresses many self-destructive coping methods and causes more pain for the parent and the rest of the extended family. Alcoholism, drug addiction, reckless behaviors, and even cancers can destroy a person during their years of misery, and can be debilitating if you don't "check yourself before you wreck yourself." The standard phrase that I share when meeting a new grieving parent, sibling, or person is, "Be gentle with yourself."

That phrase is especially relevant during the anniversaries, holidays, birthdays, and the "Angel Day" (commemoration of a loved one's passing.) The pain and sorrow caused by the negative association, around these traumatic dates, sometimes come out of nowhere, even decades after their child's death. These "sorrow dates" and specifically their child's "Angel Day" can bring emotional, psychological, and physical damage to the parent if ignored, recognized, or not correctly dealt with can bring on more unnecessary pain.

These dates sometimes come at a person from left field, even years after the death-date, and play havoc with your body. I would get migraines, stomach pain, sleepless nights, and various body aches in the early years. These pains were ten times worse than the body-pains I experienced during counseling sessions to heal the experiences from childhood abuses. There would be an "ah-ha" moment at some point during my ailments when I looked at the calendar to realize, "Oh another Mother's Day, without my boy." Then there was his death date, birthday, and holidays. Every month, there was at least one day; my body would convulse in pain and express my grief of the trauma of Anthony's loss. These ailments were very severe in the first five years of my grief journey. Over time and with recognizing the problem, I met the dates head-on and provided self-care options to ease the stress and anxiety coming my way.

Post Traumatic Stress Disorder (PTSD) is not just for soldiers. We must become aware of PTSD issues and seek professional help for the trauma in our lives. The awareness that we carry around our "grief" is vital for each person to heal after losing a child. The ability to acknowledge the need for healing is crucial for grieving parents, siblings, and family members. Each person grieves in different ways. I suggest grieving family members find unique ways to support each person's healing and grief journey. **Be Gentle With Yourselves!**

Not all counselors are the same, either. Get the help of a professional who specializes in "family grief." You and your family deserve to find joy again and live with love and happiness. We all do!

Not everyone in your life will be able to share the "grief journey" with you. I had friends drop out of my life after the death of my son. The first sign of trouble was before I moved back to Arizona from New Jersey. I was walking down a grocery store aisle and saw one of my fiancé's acquaintances at the other end of the aisle. We made eye contact; she and her family whispered something, spun around, and walked away.

I felt alone and unsupported in my grief during the early days after Anthony died. At the time, the company I worked for, Bridan Technologies, was in the computer consulting business, and the bubble was bursting on the tech world. They laid-off one-third of the programmers. As the program manager, my job was not safe, either. Compassionate Friends warned me not to make any major life decisions (moving, changing jobs, divorce) during the first year of a significant loss. My decision to move back to Phoenix was essential for me, and I was determined to do it. I took on the entire major "no-no's" and traveled back to Phoenix.

My recent engagement with Steve was now "hanging in the air." I couldn't stay in New Jersey, and I needed to start something to honor my son. My heart shattered from my son's loss, and I couldn't comprehend the depths of my sorrow. I had so many mixed-up feelings, and I couldn't see what the future would bring. My biggest and only desire was to honor my son.

Steve was an only child. He also never had children of his own. Steve was born and raised in Little Ferry, New Jersey, and still lived in the same house where he grew up. He had work and family obligations in New Jersey. For him to come with me was not possible. He would be miserable in Arizona. We shared a few visits, but he didn't feel comfortable moving to Arizona with me.

9/11 happened just fourteen months after Anthony's death. Steve was a volunteer firefighter in New Jersy. Many of his firefighter-brothers died on 9/11, and he had sadness and his own "grief journey" to process. We drifted apart and went our separate ways.

Before Anthony died, I reconnected with a family friend, Joy Rockwell. Joy was the daughter of Carol Massey. Carol was one of my favorite bosses in my career. She became my mentor and guided me to get my GED and go back to school for some college classes.

When I met Joy in 1981, we were attending the wedding of her sister, Lisa. Anthony was Lisa's ring-bearer.

When Joy and I reconnected in 1999, she was on a business trip to New York City. Joy and I met for dinner. We found a great little Italian pizza joint close to the Broadway show we had chosen, Les Miserable. At the end of the fabulous play, we both cried and bonded over our tears.

We cried more tears together after Anthony died on the last day of July 2000. By 2002, Joy had moved back to Phoenix and we reconnected. She agreed to be on the ABF Board from its inception. Joy continues to support all of our extensive programs. She comes to our heart-screenings, helps train our volunteers, and advocates for ABF in every way possible. Joy's robust career connected ABF to American Express for an influx of a substantial volunteer force.

Additionally, their "AMEX Give 2Gether" program bolstered by employee payroll deductions and matching grants by American Express has been a rock of support for ABF. As volunteers, the American Express employees come to our screening events and open house events. This program allows grant funds for the American Express employees' time and support through American Express giving. Through this connection, ABF empowers each American Express employee to become an advocate for heart health in youth. Joy is truly a "joy" in my life.

By 2013 with the American Express Employee Volunteer Program gifts Joy brought to ABF, the Reese Family of enthusiastic volunteers, Julie, Mike, Lauren, and Kyleigh, joined ABF. The girls were still in high school; they seemed to enjoy the ECG stations technology challenges. After several experiences in local ABF Cardiac Screening Days, Julie became a passionate ABF Board Member. Today, Julie continues to support ABF with her time, treasure, and talents. I am eternally grateful to Julie and her family, thank you so much for all you do to forward the mission of ABF.

Over the years, I have made many good friends through my connections with ABF. One of my unique and favorite friends is Laurie Scott, whom I met through Joy. Laurie was Joy's neighbor and started volunteering at ABF Heart-Screening events in 2011. Laurie brings light and love to our events and supports us during screenings and fundraising. We usually find her hosting the registration station at our Arizona ABF Cardiac Screening Day events. Laurie is one of our "seasoned" volunteers. Our returning volunteers who attend multiple events bring knowledge and warmth to these high school heart-screening days. "Seasoned" volunteers help ease the training learning curve in our Heart-Screening events. As well, having several "seasoned" volunteers reduces the training burden to our event coordinators. I appreciate Laurie's expertise and support upfront at the registration station of the screening events. Additionally, she retired from her retail job a few years ago and now supports our back-office mailing efforts. I genuinely value Laurie and all the volunteers who support our cause to "screen young hearts and save young lives!"

I met Wendy Dolan through my best friend at the time, Diane, at the Unity of Phoenix church in 2004. Wendy and I became closer through the Unity of Phoenix Chaplain Program in late 2005. Over the years, Wendy became my prayer chaplain, and we prayed together a lot. Wendy never had children, but she had a big heart for small children and loved life. Wendy was an enthusiastic volunteer for ABF and our screenings. She also volunteered as our Human Resource Officer. She helped us with grants and policies that we needed to create over the years. Tragically, Wendy died unexpectedly in March 2019. She will forever be in my heart as a dear friend, an "Angel on Earth," now in Heaven. I am deeply grateful for my friendship with her, and I miss her hugs and laughter.

Many people have made an impact on my life and the life of ABF. Since Anthony's death, there are not enough pages or words to describe all the meetings and connections made to benefit our cause. There have been wonderful medical supporters, doctors, technicians, and other people who all come together to share in the joy to "screen young hearts and save young lives!" I am forever grateful for each person who has made this "grief journey" a pathway towards "Damage Control" and the support of other grieving parents.

CHAPTER EIGHTEEN

Connections in Kansas

I would be remiss if I did not tell you about two dear Kansas friends I met on a flight from Newark to Kansas City, Missouri, in 1999. My consulting job came with a few rewards, such as first-class upgrades on AmericaWest flights, because of all the miles I flew back then. I met Karen Nations and Steve Koenig when I was living in New Jersey, and my consulting contractor was sending me home to Arizona every other weekend. Earlier in that fateful week a year before Anthony's death, I had corresponded with Karen via email. She was a KSU Alumni, and the New York City Watch-party coordinator. She shared with me that a "watch-party" would take place in a Manhattan bar to watch KSU football, but she wouldn't be there the following weekend, as she was going to Manhattan, Kansas, for the game. I was new to college football, and I wasn't sure what a "watch-party" was and why people would be in a bar in Manhattan when the game took place in the football stadium. I must not have heard the part about Manhattan, "New York." LOL!

On that flight back to Kansas, I did get an upgrade to first-class. That was a real treat for me! Steve Koenig occupied the first-class seat next to me. I was wearing my Kansas State University Football sweatshirt, and Mr. Koenig commented on it. We started chatting about football, and I shared with him that my son was on the K-State football team, the position he played, the number on his jersey and all the gushing "proud mom" stuff. Steve Koenig had played football at Missouri Mid-Western State University (MMSU) just a few years prior. He seemed entertained by our conversation.

By the time we got through our first chat, the flight attendant was ready for the safety announcements.

"Welcome to your AmericaWest flight to Lincoln, Nebraska!"

Well, that got my attention, and I shouted, "Kansas City!" and so did one other passenger in first class: Karen Nations. The flight attendant corrected herself to the jeers of the cabin. Later in the flight, Karen introduced herself, and I squealed, "We have been chatting on email, I am Sharon Bates!" Of course, we talked about football and the KSU band. For that game, I was getting my tickets through the KSU band director. Karen had been in the Kansas State University band during her years in college. She explained, "Those were the years that people would go to the games to watch the band!" We both laughed because it was true.

I introduced Karen to Steve Koenig. It was like a KSU tailgate party, which was still a new experience for me. I exchanged contact information with Steve Koenig. He assured me he would be watching the game.

Our flight landed; we went our separate ways. I shared several additional flights with Steve Koenig between Kansas and New Jersey. Each time we connected and talked about football.

At that game, as I explained in my conversation with Karen, I sat next to the band. The first half of play was exciting, during halftime, I was walking up the aisle and who should I see coming towards me? It was none other than Karen Nations. "What are you doing here?" I questioned, "I thought you were going to be at the watch party!"

Karen laughed, "No, the watch party is in Manhattan, New York!" Then we both laughed again!

A few weeks later, I joined Karen and a group of "Purple People" (K-State supporters) at the New York City Kansas State University Football watch-party. Karen and I became fast friends, and that football season, we enjoyed several "watch-parties" together. She was the alumni coordinator, and she knew a lot about Kansas State University, and where the best places to eat were in Manhattan, Kansas, and some in New York City!

I introduced Karen to my fiancé, Steve Iurato. We all had dinner one night, and Karen showed us pictures of the girls she planned to adopt from Russia. She was a successful attorney and had never been married, so adoption seemed a good fit for Karen. A few months later, we celebrated Karen's arrival of her adopted daughters from Russia, Elena (Lainey), and Polina (Polly.)

As the girls grew up, they became familiar with Anthony's stories and soon became volunteers at the KSU ABF Heart-Screening events. Almost every year we hosted a screening in Kansas, the Nations family volunteered. I was able to watch their family grow and mature. They even visited me in Arizona when they traveled across the country. I celebrated with Lainey after she had a little beautiful baby boy named Phoenix. Karen's daughter Polly went to Kansas State University to follow her mother's example. Polly is quite the young woman, competed in several pageants such as the Miss Kansas Pageant, and spoke on ending domestic violence on campuses everywhere. It is truly a joy to witness family love and connect with beautiful people through our ABF Screenings.

During a trip to Kansas in 2004, I searched for more support for the Cardiac Screening program we had at KSU. Coach Bill Snyder had directed me to speak with the people in the KSU Sports Communication Department (SCD). I made my way to the SCD of the KSU Athletic Department in the Bramlage Coliseum basement. The room was faintly dark, as I had just come inside from the bright sunny Kansas day. Sitting at the first desk was a perky woman with short gray curly hair.

"Good morning, How can I help you?" she questioned.

"Hello, my name is Sharon Bates . . ." I started.

I didn't have to tell her anymore. She squealed. Most people who know Shirley Serrault understand that her energy is always so bubbly and enthusiastic. She volunteers, in an instant, for causes that touch her heart. We became fast friends and helped connect ABF to additional programs and people in Manhattan, Kansas.

Over the years, Shirley and her husband Corky invited me to stay with them in their home next to Tuttle Creek Lake. It is always very peaceful, and I had many warm visits at the Serrault homestead. There was usually a fun cookout with friends and family at the Serrault home after our KSU ABF Heart-Screening events.

One of my initial friends in Kansas was Marie Dellen. Over the years, she suffered poor health, and during our many years of friendship, she lost her husband of sixty-five years. Years later, Marie went into assisted living and slipped into her final years of dementia, and eventually transitioned to eternal rest. I will miss the talks and the laughter I had with Marie. I vividly remember her great mixture of cereal and candies called "Bird-Seed." She would donate the salty-sugary concoction to groups of athletes and coaches. Everyone adored her, and she loved her KSU Wildcat Family. Marie unselfishly gave of herself to Kansas State. She was dearly loved and genuinely missed by many.

Just a month after Anthony's death, my fiancé, Steve Iurato, and I flew from Kansas back to New Jersey. I spotted Steve Koenig at the gate, ready to board the plane. I asked my fiancé to approach Mr. Koenig and share the news about Anthony. I wasn't sure that he had heard about his death. I was right; he was shaken and very sad. A few weeks later, Mr. Koenig and I connected by phone and invited us to dinner. During our meal, I shared a dream I had of hosting a fundraiser dinner, where the places at the table would go for hundreds of dollars. I wish non-profit fundraising came that easy as in my dreams.

Steve Koenig and I stayed in touch through my move back to Phoenix and the growth of ABF. In 2006, a few years after the foundation launch, I received a panic call from him, "Sharon, I was diagnosed with HCM. I don't know what to do." Hypertrophic Cardiomyopathy (HCM), an enlarged heart, was the same condition Anthony died from in July 2000. I helped him calm down and told him about Lisa Salberg in New Jersey. Together we went to her website and found an HCM Center of Excellence in New York City. Dr. Mark Sherrid took excellent care of my friend, Mr. Koenig.

Six months later, I received another phone call from Steve Koenig. He blurted, "Sharon, you saved my life!" He explained the care he had received from Dr. Sherrid, the doctor who had performed the heart surgery for Steve's HCM. The operation reduced Steve's symptoms of heart disease. He went on to detail, with great gratitude, how his health had significantly improved. On a subsequent trip to Arizona, I asked him to be an ABF Board member. He has served dutifully for many years and continues to be my friend to this day.

One of my first connections to the Kansas State University Football office was Joan Friederich. Joan worked at KSU Football long before Coach Snyder took the job as the head football coach. She was his "gate-keeper" and my "all-knowing connector" to Coach Snyder. If you needed something from Coach, first, you had to go through Joan. She gave me advice and support that no one could dispute. She loved all the football players and treated them all with so much admiration and respect, and she was a sweetheart to me. Joan also grieved for my son.

I remember her stories of some of the different K-State football players. The young men would come into her office to have a piece of candy from the large bowl on her desk. It was their way of connecting with Joan and staying in step with the program. She shared with me her own "Anthony stories." He had come to KSU in early January 1999. It was winter, but he did the house-hunting research and found an apartment. She was proud of his ability and maturity to handle the new experience of Kansas State University Football. Joan told me she never saw Anthony in the coach's office for discipline or bad grades. Her recollections of my son made me so proud of him. To me and the people that knew him, Anthony was a good boy!

In the early weeks after Anthony died, I would get surprise, laminated, newspaper clippings about Anthony in the mail. On a trip back to Kansas, I asked Joan about the mystery mail, and she explained about her cousin, Marie Dellen, who worked for Kansas State Bank as the community-relations person. Among some of her duties, Marie would cut out newspaper clippings of bank customers. She asked for my address to send the clippings of Anthony to me. I drove over to the branch, where she worked, to meet this wonderful woman.

Marie was a stout woman of mature years. She was maybe five feet even and had a great laugh. When we met, her eyes filled with tears, and we hugged. I didn't know that Anthony and Marie had already met, but she immediately shared the "tractor pull story" at the Riley County Fair. This event occurred the weekend before Anthony died.

Some Kansas State University Football players and team captains were usually out in the community for events as allowed by the "compliance" department. On this occasion, Jason Kazar, KSU Linebacker, and one of the team captains wasn't able to fulfill his obligation to the Riley County Fair event. He asked Anthony to go in his place. Of course, Anthony agreed, and that was where he met Marie Dellen. Marie was in charge of the "tractor pull" contest. Young children five through twelve years old participate in this event at the fair — riding peddle-tractors with weights on the back guided by their age category and timed. The KSU Football players were the cheerleaders of the event. The football player would walk alongside the tractors and competitors, cheering them on to the finish line.

The KSU Compliance Office also approved a benefit that Marie offered to the football players: a home-cooked meal shortly after their "cheerleading" volunteer job. Marie loved to cook tasty old-fashioned meals. After the event concluded, Marie informed Anthony about the upcoming meal. He was so excited to learn of some home-cooked chow that he picked up Marie and twirled her around in glee. The next day, Anthony died, and Marie was heartbroken; she never made him that fried-chicken dinner.

Marie and I wept over her telling me that story. As soon as she got the pictures back from the developer (pre-digital cameras), she mailed me copies of Anthony's precious moments of his last night in Kansas. I cherish every photo of my son in his glory, supporting the community where he lived, played, and worked.

On my numerous trips to Kansas, Marie invited me to stay at her home. Of course, I took her up on her offer because hotels were beginning to put a dent in my travel budget. Besides, Marie was fun to hang out and laugh with as we enjoyed the town of Manhattan together. On most of my visits with Marie, we would share at least one meal at the Little Apple Brewery and, on occasion, breakfast at the Early Edition. Marie knew some great places to enjoy our meals in Manhattan. Marie invited me to church services with her when my travel plans allowed a Sunday morning service. She would share her life stories in Kansas, and the activities she enjoyed through Kansas State University sports. I was able to share some fun life stories about Anthony with her.

Over the years, Marie helped me connect to other folks in Manhattan, Kansas. When ABF hosted several fundraising events there, Marie would help join us in the community's generous businesses. She knew a lot about the town and the companies to approach for support with our ABF Golf Tournaments, fundraising opportunities, and donating prizes during our heart-screening events.

I also befriended a beautiful couple in Manhattan, named Larry and Donna Schlappi. They sent me a card right after Anthony died and offered their home to me on my trips to Kansas. I would regularly switch staying between Marie's house and that of Larry and Donna. Larry and Donna introduced me to their friends. They would connect me to fantastic KSU athletes who had been in college before and after Anthony died. Their house and their life were all "K-State Purple!" Hence, there seems to be a "Purple People" theme to all my friends in Manhattan, Kansas. That is why I chose to use royal purple as the ABF colors. We are a family.

As a Unity of Phoenix Chaplain, each of us had to "hold space" (which means to hold an intention of prayerful energy) at a minimum of one church service per month. There were many weekends I was at all three church services. The warmth and prayer connection I received during the Unity services was magical. Moments of pure inspiration and guidance came to me during the church services and in meditation.

In early 2003, I had the honor to hear the angelic voice of Susan Kay Wyatt one weekend. She sang a song called "Somewhere Sacred Here!" that gave me goosebumps, or "God-bumps," as some would say. After the service, I shared my Anthony story (elevator speech style – 2 minutes or less) with her through my tears, asking her permission to use her music track for our ABF educational video titled, "What is HCM?" She graciously agreed, and I enjoy her music and our friendship today.

CHAPTER NINETEEN

Cardiac Safety Research Consortium (CSRC)

In early 2015, I sent a message to Carlton Cleland, a good friend I met through the Kansas State University ABF Heart-Screening events. He was in the medical business. I needed help in connecting ABF to research entities. Carlton was an Electrocardiogram (ECG/EKG) sales representative for Mortara Instrument Services. He and I became friends around 2006 when I searched for ECG tests to add to our screening program. He was knowledgeable, helpful, and a joy to work with, and he became a volunteer at many of the KSU ABF Heart-Screening Events. Later on, Carlton met up with ABF at several Colorado heart-screening events to volunteer and support our work. He even introduced me to the Program Director, Rusty Taylor, at Washburn University, Topeka, Kansas. From 2008 until 2018, Rusty brought Washburn students to KSU screenings. They received clinical experience for their course work and offered community service to ABF.

The mission of the CSRC is as follows: "To advance scientific knowledge on cardiac safety for new and existing medical products by building a collaborative environment based upon the principles of the FDA's Critical Path Initiative as well as other public health priorities."

The purpose of the CSRC is as follows: "a public-private partnership aimed to support research into the evaluation of cardiac safety of medical products." One of its outputs is the publication of consensus white papers with participation of experts from industry, academia, and regulatory agencies. These position papers usually cover challenging areas of cardiovascular safety, describing what is known and unknown, and propose paths forward to address knowledge gaps. These white papers are not regulatory guidance's, nor are they intended to serve as de facto guidance documents.

I approached the Cardiac Safety Research Consortium (CSRC), and their connections to Duke University research. In our initial meeting in May 2015, the CSRC flew me out to Duke University, and there was a comprehensive conference call with the CSRC team and Darren Sudman. Darren and his wife, Phyllis, operate Simon's Heart in Philadelphia, Pennsylvania. In 2004, Darren and Phyllis lost their son, Simon, at seven weeks old. Simon didn't wake up from a nap due to undetected Long-QT Syndrome, which causes irregular heart rhythms and is known to cause Sudden Cardiac Deaths. Phyllis was later diagnosed with Long QT and was implanted with a cardiac defibrillator to protect her from experiencing a Sudden Cardiac Arrest (SCA). Darren met me through Parent Heart Watch and learned how to host heart-screening events during one of the ABF Arizona events. As an ABF Trained Team, I invited Darren to participate in the CSRC meetings because their screening program had become an excellent example of a data-driven experience to prove that children have heart disease and prevent SCA in youth.

From 2015 through 2017, I met monthly with these doctors, researchers, pharmaceutical partners in hopes of building a research network and funding source for the non-profits doing the majority of screenings in the U.S. Many of the researchers within CSRC wanted "long-term studies." Within the first year of attempting to work with the CSRC, I introduced them to Parent Heart Watch (PHW) leader, Martha Lopez-Anderson. I was so excited about the prospects of research I tried to persevere through the arduous research process. I even shared my enthusiasm with Coach Bill Snyder, and he introduced me to Merton Hanks, Director of NFL Operations, of the National Football League. In turn, Mr. Hanks put me in touch with the NFL Charities, and we started to work through a possible grant for the CSRC. However, the CSRC wouldn't move forward. During the three years, I partnered with the CSRC; there was NO funding, NO research, NO white paper on screening position, and NO cooperation. I turned over the project to Martha, and I reluctantly and angrily stepped away.

Our country has an overflow of funds for "profit-making" organizations such as the NCAA, NFL, NHL, and others. Each company could help save the future of children in sports. Children make up the future players and fan-base of the myriad of sports leagues around the world. Building impactful donors for the screening programs and hosting the majority of events nationwide would be a catalyst for a national movement's sustainability. Unfortunately, the CSRC was only interested in data and finding their research niche, and not in the long-term goals of supporting the group's heart-screening endeavors. We must help screening organizations, like ABF, to make crucial differences in their communities. Support by sports organizations must be accomplished by building the bridge to garner future backing for more significant events and save more lives. Both the "goodwill" and genuine satisfaction that comes from saving a young life is truly immeasurable. Take up the challenge and stand with us in the truth that all children have value in this world!

While I was in the CSRC group for three years, I learned a lot about medicine's politics. There were many "actors" vying for their time in the limelight. I feel such frustration when new "actors" come on the stage with ideas to write the next research paper and expand the research into long-term studies. Remember, I had already found research studies dating back to the early 1960s that children who play sports, can have heart disease and go into Sudden Cardiac Arrest. What new research is necessary to take action? How does new research help the children of today? The studies of the 1960s had already proved that children could suffer SCA while playing sports. There was no need to "reinvent the wheel" unless they just wanted to turn those "wheels" into profits for themselves.

There have been plenty of papers written about cardiovascular risks in children and sports. ABF has plenty of data, with more than 1 million hearts screened across the USA. What are the researchers waiting to prove? They are, in effect, researching "old news." The parents of the children who have died must take a stand and rally together against these companies profiting from the loss of children's lives. The "lack of heart" found in much of cardiac medicine continues to disturb me. Together, we will challenge these companies, industries, and programs that take advantage of children. Here is your chance to get involved in making a massive difference in the world. I will support your worthy endeavors. The more we do together the larger our global impact will be.

The Italian government and Italian medical community did it the right way by mandating through a law to require that ALL sports participants from age twelve through thirty-five be heart-healthy to participate. They reduced the rate of death by eighty-nine percent. An Italian child's heart is no different from that of an American child's heart. Heart disease may present itself differently from Italy to the U.S. However, children are still dying of HCM and other heart diseases in America, where screenings are yet NOT required! I encourage parents everywhere to stand up for the TRUTH and demand our nation to follow Italy's example. One more life lost is too many! Researchers for these large conglomerates need to throw away their egos, search their own hearts, and accept the reality of the established research of the past. Life is so short and precious to waste on the ego-centered recognition (and money) to just get "your name or your intitution's name" on the research paper.

Meanwhile, children in the U.S. will continue to die from Sudden Cardiac Arrest (SCA) until the cardiology world, sports industries, and education systems "wake up" to the TRUTH. Heart disease in children and young athletes' is a real issue. Preventable Sudden Cardiac Death (SCD) can happen through obligatory heart-screenings and preparation for the SCA emergencies.

Parents, search your heart, and step into the fight with us. We need all the enthusiastic support we can muster to save the next child after that! The next person protected by the Anthony Bates Foundation or the ABF Trained Teams across the U.S. could be your child or someone you know and love.

Over the years, I wanted to give up on our ABF Heart-Screening Programs countless times. I would take time off, usually over the holidays or summer break, when children were not in school. Unfortunately, I would become enraged with the next news story about a young life lost to a cardiac malady, when school activities and sports resumed without requiring youngsters to have their hearts screened. These stories refueled my passion, as Anthony's spirit prodded me to "keep going!"

When Anthony was a child, and we would take road trips, one of our games in the car was the "alphabet game" and other similar games. We would search for signs and license plates for the letters needed next in the game. I still have this habit when I am driving to search for signs and license plates. After Anthony died, I would see the number "91" in phone numbers, on signs, or on license plates. Recognizing that number raised a smile to my lips that Anthony was watching me, or riding in the car. Even though these phenomena occur, the games we played brought more awareness of his number to my psyche. I anticipate seeing "91's" everywhere, which causes me to "see more of them." With each "91," I feel closer to Anthony's spirit. That is another reason why I added a "91" to the ABF logo. The number recognition continues to motivate me to do more screening events, place more AED's in schools, and rejoice to save one or more lives through heart-screening events. Anthony is always looking out for me; I can feel it in my heart.

CHAPTER TWENTY

Free is not Free

Free is never free! Those free pencils you might have gotten in school came to you courtesy of the average taxpayer. The only things that are free in this world are the air we breathe and our hearts' love. On the other hand, does that come with a cost, too? I did not start the Anthony Bates Foundation to become wealthy or affluent. ABF grew out of me wanting to honor my son's memory and a love for the then 64 million children in the U.S., now over 74 million. They are all breathing that free air right here, right now! ABF plans keep them breathing that air!

In the early years, most of the work around prevention and protection to children from Sudden Cardiac Arrest (SCA) we did through screenings gave me an outlet for the grief I dealt with daily from the loss of my son. Then, the "grief-fog" lifted and I saw the results and appreciation from parents and families for saving thousands of lives.

In the first years of screening events that ABF offered the public, the screenings were done "by appointment" and "through donation." By 2005, fifty percent of people that made appointments did not show up. There were volunteers lined up to help the masses, but volunteers often stopped signing up when people "skipped out" on their appointment. The dilemma prompted the necessity of charging minimal and reasonable fees for heart-screening appointments. ABF still charges nominal fees today well under the rate of expense and market value for these services. Additionally, nearing 2021, ABF continues to provide free heart-screening tests to volunteers during our large high school or college screening events.

CHAPTER TWENTY-ONE

Saving Sam!

A thirteen-year-old boy named Sam was on the way to his soccer game one fall day in 2014. His mother and father, Sandra and Darryl, decided to bring him to an Anthony Bates Foundation heart-screening in North Phoenix. Sam didn't make it to his soccer game that day because our ABF team discovered a severe hidden heart issue. He had no symptoms and no family history.

Two weeks later, he was in Phoenix Children's Hospital, receiving life-saving surgery to fix his heart. Sam had a fixable heart condition called Wolff-Parkinson-White (WPW). We are happy to report Sam is heart-healthy and back on the playing field. Now Sam and his parents are outspoken advocates and volunteers for the Foundation.

Our Anthony Bates Foundation's work is unique, filling a dangerous healthcare gap currently only testing children with symptoms.

After Sam healed from his heart surgery, Sam and his family became advocates of our program. Sam and his parents volunteered on several occasions at an area high school heart-screening event as Sam made his way through grade school to high school and now college. In 2016, at one such event, Sam operated the laptop, and his parents were putting electrodes on the participants in the boy's ECG station. That day, ABF, with the help of the VanDusen family, found another young man with the same condition that we had discovered in Sam, years before. Sometimes the ripple in the pond expands out to the ocean through the people we directly impact. I am grateful to know Sam and his family and thankful for their continued support in "screening young hearts and saving young lives!"

CHAPTER TWENTY-TWO

The $600,000

Vacation

By Phyllis Sudman

With permission from the author, Phyllis Sudman, the following story is reprinted from April 26, 2016, blog entry from Huff Post Life. The blog post illustrates both the astronomical, unnecessary costs that can burden a family falling victim to a Sudden Cardiac Arrest to one of their children. The author is the co-founder of Simon's Heart, created after the Sudden Cardiac Death of her seven-week-old son, Simon.

Phyllis reports, "This vacation was out of control. Their room was $5,900 a night. The helicopter ride cost $36,347. They spent more than $1,000 a day on drugs. It was like nothing I'd ever heard of before."

Phyllis continues, "Last summer, my friends took their family to Virginia. They rented a nice house with a pool -- a prerequisite for three kids under ten. One beautiful day hanging out around the pool, they turned around and found one of their children at the bottom, unconscious.

"For twenty-six minutes, they performed CPR and waited for the paramedics to arrive. For twenty-six minutes, he didn't breathe, and his heart didn't pump. When the first responders arrived, they shocked his heart with an Automatic External Defibrillator (AED) device.

"Sudden cardiac arrest may be sudden, as the name suggests, in which case, there is little that can be done to prevent it. However, some studies indicate that most children who experience sudden cardiac arrest have at least one warning sign. An underlying heart condition causes Sudden Cardiac Arrest. Most of these conditions can be detected with an electrocardiogram (ECG/EKG).

"What began as an idyllic family vacation turned into a nightmare. We thought Timmy, a family friend, had no chance of survival due to the statistics on Sudden Cardiac Arrest, drowning, and resuscitation.

"Timmy was in a coma for six days. During his hospital stay, he was diagnosed with a heart condition called Long QT Syndrome, a potentially-fatal arrhythmia that disrupts the heartbeat. Before his discharge, he received an implantable cardioverter-defibrillator (ICD)."

Phyllis continued with her own story, "In 2005, my son, Simon, died from this condition. Following his death, I was diagnosed with the same condition. It is responsible for up to fifteen percent of all SIDS deaths. It is one of a handful of conditions that makes cardiac arrest the leading cause of student-athletes' death.

"As with my situation, Timmy's family didn't know about their son's heart condition because children don't get EKG exams. American Heart Association and American College of Cardiology, the two organizations, decided three decades ago that asking students twelve questions about their hearts and family history was good enough. Timmy is nine. He has had that exam and was asked those questions at least three times. It is safe to assume that most children who collapse and die from Sudden Cardiac

Arrest have passed this AHA/ACC exam. In the medical world, that is called a "false negative."

"One of the major arguments against screening kids' hearts is the cost. For a minute, aside from the fact that a tiny group of physicians from these two organizations is claiming that your child is not worth the exam's value. Instead, let's look at Timmy's experience and explore economics.

"Timmy's eighteen-day cardiac arrest episode cost $596,806. Put another way; it cost more than a half a million dollars to save one nine-year-old child's life.

"Alternatively, Timmy could have gotten a $25 ECG/EKG exam before his vacation. He could have discovered his heart condition, go on a beta-blocker, which costs about $5 per month, and enjoyed his Virginia family vacation. What sounds more appealing to you?

"Proponents of heart-screenings suggest that the cost can be as low as $15. The opponents of heart-screenings indicated that it is as high as $260. Let's ignore both sides of the argument since they each have their own biases, and look at some medical institutions providing this service.

"Peace Health charges $50 for youth cardiac screening. Beaumont Hospital has offered the screening for as low as $10 per student. By way of reference, Italy, which mandated heart-screenings for all children, puts the cost around $60 per child. By the way, Italy reduced the incidents of sudden cardiac arrest by eighty-nine percent."

"Since Peace Health seems to have found a sustainable and scalable way to screen our youth, let's use their number.

"Take Timmy's medical bills of $597,000 and divide them by the cost of one youth heart-screening ($50). The result is 11,940. For the amount of money used to save one Timmy from sudden cardiac arrest, we could have screened 11,940 students at these two institutions.

"This doesn't solve our problem, though. There are more than 11,940 students in this country. So, let's start with the highest-risk population -- student-athletes. We do this all the time in medicine. It is a way to protect the most vulnerable and learn in the process.

"There are 8 million student-athletes in the United States. To screen this population (at $50 per athlete), we would need $400 million. That seems like a whole lot of money until you think about Timmy.

"Every year in this country, almost 400,000 people die from sudden cardiac arrest. The number of deaths is more than breast cancer, lung cancer, and AIDS combined. Isn't it likely that out of that number, 670 would be kids like Timmy? If so, we just spent $400 million. We spend way more than that because nationally, we only save about eleven percent of people who experience sudden cardiac arrest. That means we are trying to save way more than 400,000 people a year and spending much more money.

"Shouldn't we opt for the alternative? Shouldn't we screen our children to get a baseline of their heart; discover conditions that could be life-threatening in the short term; discover conditions that could be life-shortening in the long run; or prevent cardiovascular disease? Doesn't it behoove us to know as much about our hearts as early as possible? It is the #1 cause of death, remember?"

"Timmy checked back into the hospital in February 2016. He stayed there for sixteen days. Two surgeries later, he got a new ICD. This "vacation" cost hundreds of thousands of dollars. Timmy's experience was closer to $1 million. We could have screened a few more kids, probably."

Phyllis professes, "My son, Simon, was worth everything to me. He saved my life. I discovered my heart condition because we didn't discover his condition. In 2012, at a 'Simon's Heart' screening, Whitney Jones was found to have Long QT Syndrome. Soon after that, her mother, Rayna, was diagnosed with it, too. No one had to die. That's how it should work."

CHAPTER TWENTY-THREE

How Can We Make a Difference?

In 2019, more than 325,000 people died from Sudden Cardiac Arrest in the U.S. Estimates from the Institute of Medicine (IOM)[3] claim more than 12,000 were children. Why, as a nation, are we not alarmed by these statistics? Why are we not providing mandatory testing to help prevent these unnecessary deaths? Tests that cost less than $30 each compared to $1300 for the COVID-19 test. After the COVID-19 pandemic is over, we need to focus on prevention of disease. Particularly, focus for our country should be on prevention of Sudden Cardiac Deaths from SCA!

The medical industry does not view the prevention of Sudden Cardiac Death as a priority. The pharmaceutical industry, as related to the CSRC to build safer heart drugs, continues to make money on heart drugs and heart devices. However, there are many more

---

[3] Strategies to Improve Cardiac Arrest Survival: A Time to Act, Robert Graham, Margaret A. McCoy, and Andrea M. Schultz, Institute of Medicine of the National Academies, ISBN 978-0-309-37199-5 | DOI 10.17226/21723, June 2015

patients to save if screenings were readily available. In 1996, the American Heart Association (AHA) lowered testing standards for the elitist groups like the NCAA. Today, many countries and global sports leagues require heart testing. Unfortunately, other major U.S. youth sports organizations turn a "blind eye" to the liability of being unprepared for an SCA emergency.

To protect the general population and specifically young athletes, the various sports leagues and organizations in the U.S. must take affirmative action to save lives! We need to continue to raise the issue of Sudden Cardiac Arrest by having an open dialogue among parents, coaches, school administrators, health officials, researchers, and government officials to all "get on the same page" about SCA's reality. Too many children are dying from SCA. In large part, U.S. children's deaths are due to the disregard of proven facts, by some in the medical profession, that SCA does affect thousands of youngsters yearly. To prevent hundreds, if not thousands of children's deaths, we need mandatory heart screenings.

CHAPTER TWENTY-FOUR

Finding Love Again!

Through my single years before and after Anthony died, I was floundering and failing at every relationship. The failure of all my romantic relationships with men and many of my platonic female friendships had one common denominator: me. I used Anthony as an excuse and a cover for work relationships, too. I became a "contract" worker so as not to invest in relationships at work. On many occasions, I failed miserably, superficially caring about the people I worked with, and I later hid behind my son's loss to close my heart to any other person in my life.

Life doesn't come with an instruction book. Losing a child doesn't come with an instruction book. Sadly, it took me years and many more tears to face the truth. There are books on divorce recovery and grief recovery that made me realize that the one common factor in all my failed relationships continued to be me.

How could I get on with my life when I held onto the pain so tightly? The pain of loss and abandonment was my defense mechanism to avoid emotions, especially heartfelt emotions. I had to find a way or die alone, never knowing true love, never getting my life back.

As I previously mentioned, in 2004, I had found my way to Unity of Phoenix. The prayer life I longed for was right there, and I felt at home. I was still new to my grief, only four years in, and I felt by no means ready to heal my heart.

Fast forward to the 2016 Memorial Day weekend. I searched for a movie buddy, and Laurie, Joy, and Wendy were all out of town or unavailable for my ritual. I went on Facebook and saw a picture of my best friend, Joy, and a group of people at a live music event the night before. Another mutual friend from the Unity of Phoenix church, Kevin Gregory, posted the group picture on Facebook. His photos are always great, and that one caught my eye. I spotted Will Maier in the image. I remembered his sweet smile, humor, and friendship. I thought to myself, *"Maybe Will is available to go to the movies with me."* I ferreted out his phone number from my contact list, called him, and found out he was free, and we reconnected.

Here is Will's version of how our "love story" transpired:

A Love Story ... Sharon and Will

By Will Maier

"Once upon a time... there was a girl named Sharon and a boy named Will who met at Unity of Phoenix church in 2004 and became friends. Though each was involved with other people, they had a special bond because they had suffered tragedies regarding their respective children. Sharon's son, Anthony, died suddenly at age 20. Will's two young children had been turned against him by their mother in what is known as "parent alienation syndrome" (a situation that goes under-reported and affects many divorced parents, especially fathers). Sharon and Will's paths crossed several times over the next six years, through various parties and social events, at their homes and particularly at Sharon's non-profit office. They laughed a lot together and became platonic friends. About 2007 or 2008, they both happened to attend a mutual friend's wedding. As fate would have it, they were waiting, not so patiently, in their respective gender bathroom lines when Will said (paraphrasing here) prophetically, "If things don't work out between Diane and me, we should get together. I think we could have a lot of fun!" Will knew things were going downhill fast with Diane due to a severe personal problem she had and refused to deal with to get help. He was not suggesting to Sharon anything more than literally "going out" for a fun activity. Will doesn't remember how exactly Sharon responded. Except that, she didn't take it the "wrong way." Will had just realized how much he had always enjoyed her company. Well, Will did end his marriage in October 2010, though he didn't run into Sharon again for several more years. Sharon settled into a series of unfulfilling dating experiences, as did Will. However, both wanted a committed, loving, spiritual relationship with someone who could also make their toes curl with a kiss. Fast forward to Memorial Day Weekend, 2016. Sharon happened to be on Facebook, and saw a picture of Will, and gave him a call. Well, Will WASN'T doing anything because he was burned out on boring coffee dates. Sharon, through "Divine Intervention," (since there are "no accidents in the universe"), picked up the phone and YES, asked Will to go see a movie with her. Who doesn't love an assertive woman like that? Though "The Date" as it is in the annals of history, was purely 'friendly,' they had such a good time they did redo the very next day for another (inconsequential) flick. They went back to Will's apartment to watch the recorded NBA Finals, and things started to become less platonic. Presto-chango thus started "The Relationship." What was the chance of THAT happening? (100%, because it happened)."

Will has my heart now, for over four years! With him in my life, I feel love again, and together life is more meaningful. He supports me in my ABF work and truly understands the shadow on my heart, Anthony. We comfort each other through the challenges of living in this

Musée de l'Orangerie, Paris, 2018

world. I am blessed to have Will in my life. He is the most sensitive and caring man I have ever known.

We have fun together, as he alluded to in his story. We love to travel, having been to San Diego in 2016, Montana, and Yellowstone in 2017. Then, in 2018, we traveled to Europe visiting France, Belgium, Holland, Switzerland, Italy, and Spain. We were planning a trip to Hawaii later this year – until the COVID-19 pandemic put a pause on our journey, which we hope to pursue in 2021. The next trip is his gift to me for taking care of him for four months before and after his hip replacement surgery. We also enjoy doing things together like going to the gym, movies, dining out, discussing current events, politics, spirituality, and listening to classic rock 'n roll. Will sang in a band for a couple of years, and I enjoyed going to their gigs. He makes me laugh! I call him my "Clown Ninja" (he's been doing martial arts for nearly 50 years.) Our laughter together has become one of our many joys! We have had sad moments, though. In 2019, two of our dear fur-babies, Murphy (cat) and Hershey (dog), "crossed over the rainbow bridge." Additionally, our dear friend, Wendy, died suddenly. She was just fifty-eight years young. As I said earlier, life doesn't come with a playbook, chapters one through ten. Life is a journey of all the experiences we have separately and together. Through all these experiences and more, Will and I "keep going!" We continue on our path and persevere through this magical experience called life.

CHAPTER TWENTY-FIVE

Reflection

There have been many hurdles to overcome in my life. Looking back, I realize the loss of my child and the childhood that I also lost were big hurdles. The failed marriages, the education hassles, and shaky career have led me to my truths about life. Anyone reading this book has had life lessons that could take up chapters of your own story. I wrote this book because I cleared the hurdles that I faced in my life. There were times that I had to "bang my head" on many walls, but I persevered to "keep going and keep growing." This book recognizes the pain that lay hidden for years. With this book and the lessons of life I've learned, I acknowledge the people who have helped me overcome the biggest hurdle of all, the loss of my son.

None of the lessons I faced were easy. Some caused great pain and agony. Some were fun and exciting moments, but there were challenges, just like a computer language. The trick is to have the commands flow with style, and the computer would respond. Life is like a computer that doesn't always react so efficiently to our expectations, directions, desires, or dreams. We just keep trying to master the lessons and love to share our journey with the special people in our lives. We are not alone; we are a village of survivors. It often takes a village to save a life, and I am grateful to all my villagers that saved mine!

Many of the challenges I faced had another common denominator: overcoming the need to "control" life's situations. We also cannot control people or many events in life. Fortunately, aspects of my career have allowed me to learn to "let go" of all the outcomes and focus on the most critical areas. Included in these focus areas are my personal physical and spiritual health, a meaningful, loving relationship with Will, spending time with my friends, professionally continuing to "screening young hearts and saving young lives!" and writing this book, *Damage Control,* to share all of this with you.

However, there have been challenges I have faced in the past and still deal with today, going up against some organizations reluctant to advocate for mandatory heart-screening. I have been guilty of harboring anger in these circumstances, and I frequently have to remind myself to "let go and let God!" I continue to strive to heal my heart and find the "joys of life." Happiness is a choice. I get to choose how I show up today, after my life's hardest experience, losing my son twenty years ago. Although I can't change what life has thrown at me, I now have learned to choose happiness, joy, and love as my methods for "damage control!"

CHAPTER TWENTY-SIX

Saving Scott!

Scott Perry and his wife, Sheri in 2014.

At age forty-four, the ABF team of volunteers saved Scott Perry's life at one of our screenings in 2013. His high-school sweetheart and wife, Sheri, encouraged the whole family to participate in the heart-screening event when ABF came to her school. Scott came in with his son, Scotty, who had recently passed out on the playing field. It turned out that Scotty's doctor later diagnosed him with exercise-induced asthma, and his heart tests were routine through our screening. Interestingly, Scotty never had another fainting episode after the testing.

During our ABF heart-screening, the ultrasound technician tested Scott (the dad), and the technician asked Scott if he was aware that he had an aneurysm. An aneurysm occurs when part of an artery wall weakens, allowing it to balloon out or widen abnormally. Scott said, "No." Our on-site cardiologist directed Scott to see his family doctor immediately and further evaluate his medical situation. Scott made his appointments and saw the referred cardiologist, who wasn't sure that a screening test would pick up such a condition. The doctor re-tested Scott with a diagnostic ultrasound test. After reviewing the test results, the doctor scheduled for Scott to have immediate corrective surgery within two weeks to fix his heart. The cardiologist instructed Scott not to go to work, avoid strenuous activities, and wait for surgery. The surgery corrected his seven-centimeter aneurysm and made him heart-healthy.

While Scott was prepping for surgery, the nurse came in to ask questions and get him ready for the operating room. Her name was Joy Crouse, and they started chatting about his heart issue. Scott told him about the screening and of the discovered aneurysm at our recent event. Joy asked him what event. Scott replied, "Oh, you probably never heard of them. It was the Anthony Bates Foundation in Anthem a few weeks ago." Joy started to smile, "Yes, I was there that day volunteering." Scott was thrilled. He continued, "I am happy you were there. I am in good hands now. I know I am going to live!"

Wait, there is more! While Scott was having surgery, his parents arrived from Rhode Island to care for their grandchildren and support the family during Scott's recovery. On the day of Scott's surgery, his two children collected their grandparents at Sky Harbor Airport, at which time Grandpa Scott (all three Perry men have the same name) started complaining of chest pain. It turned out that he had a heart attack. The family immediately drove straight to the E.R. at the same hospital where Scott Jr. was having his surgery. Due to his timely visit, Grandpa Scott Sr.'s immediate medical attention saved his life, too. That is our "double-rainbow" story! You never know how many people will be impacted by your life until you start counting them. Thank you to the Perry family for taking everyone's heart health seriously and for attending our ABF Heart-Screening event in Anthem back in 2013.

CHAPTER TWENTY-SEVEN

Saving Andrew!

In 2010, ABF Volunteers screened Andrew's heart during our first and only screening event at Missouri Mid-Western State University (MMSU). MMSU happens to be Steve Koenig's alma mater; Steve invited ABF to share our program in St. Joseph, Missouri. That year, we dove-tailed the MMSU event with the KSU event the next weekend.

Andrew Pieper and his sister, Morgan in 2011.

We screened 285 people that day in Missouri, and Andrew was the fifth person screened. His Electrocardiogram (ECG/EKG) test came back abnormal. It turned out he had Wolff-Parkinson-White (WPW) syndrome. WPW is a fixable electrical problem in the heart that can cause a Sudden Cardiac Arrest if untreated. It is like having an extra electrical wire in the heart wall. A specialized cardiac doctor known as an electrophysiologist can detect and correct this heart problem. The next week, the doctors performed Andrew's heart surgery to repair his heart condition following the MMSU ABF Heart-Screening event.

After his surgery, I received a heartfelt thank-you from his mother, Hilary, and a separate message from his grandparents, Angela, and Tom Pieper. Before the Pieper family outpoured gratitude, it had taken me ten years to learn to accept such gratitude for "screening young hearts and saving young lives!" We had saved numerous others by that time, but I must have had a block in my soul that wouldn't let me feel the overwhelming acknowledgement from all the gracious people. For many years, I blocked out my worthiness of the appreciation they bestowed upon me. I have now learned to accept kindness from the families who receive life-saving news from ABF. Still, every screening event and every life saved is truly a lesson in humility. When ABF offers heart screens, these tests provided at each event will protect young lives from the risks of Sudden Cardiac Death.

CHAPTER TWENTY-EIGHT

Saving Reece!

**Coach Bill Snyder, Reece Wewer
and Sharon Bates, 2017**

In 2016, at the KSU ABF Heart-Screening event in Manhattan, Kansas, we found a problem with a young man's screening tests, Reece Wewer. He had Wolff-Parkinson-White (WPW), the same condition as Andrew and Sam. His family is grateful to the screenings, and the opportunity to have their son's heart condition corrected. Not everyone with a heart condition has to carry a death sentence. Healthcare options are available after a successful screening!

Coincidently, another young man mentioned several times in my book, Jason Kazar, is also a good family friend of the Wewer family parents, Paula and Randy. Jason also allowed Anthony to go to the July 2000 Riley County Fair "tractor pull" and spoke at Anthony's funeral for all the KSU football team. Some say now we are only three degrees of separation from knowing everyone on this planet. Is that due to Facebook, Kansas State University Football, or the Anthony Bates Foundation? I pick the ABF!

CHAPTER TWENTY-NINE

Saving Tayler!

Tayler Pruett and Sharon Bates, 2019

In 2013, at the same ABF Heart-Screening event in Anthem, Arizona, where ABF saved Scott Perry, ABF also saved Tayler Pruett. Tayler was twelve-years-old at the time. I had not received information about her outcome until several years later when she was a senior in high school. In January 2019, I received a small email message from Tayler, asking for permission to gift ABF the proceeds of her high-school charity competition, the "Mr. BC Pageant." We connected during the months before the pageant at Boulder Creek High School. Her mother, Jessie, and I embraced the night of the pageant and shared a few words of gratitude and love. Meetings like that are very emotional and sometimes all that is necessary is a hug and a "thank-you!" The rest is a heart-to-heart connection!

Every child in this world deserves a chance to live a healthy, prosperous life! Just like Andrew, Sam, Reece, Tayler, and even young adults like Scott. Families would be devastated if any one of these precious lives had ended suddenly. Taking steps to prevent such tragedies has become my life's work, honor, and joy.

Ask any person saved through one of our Anthony Bates Foundation Heart-Screenings, if their life was worth saving. We know the answer would be a resounding **YES!**

CHAPTER THIRTY

Educating Parents and Medical Communities

For the sustainability of ABF, the summer of 2016, was hard! ABF ran out of money waiting for funding sources through our research connections. I was also attempting to sell my house to pay off my accumulated debt from very little and more often no compensation for screening youth. The two staff members I had hired at ABF months earlier where tasked to fundraise and assist in our research partnership. We all were poised to build up for the Duke University and the CSRC database project, which regrettably had to be "let go!" I had to dig in and make some hard decisions to keep the foundation operational. I had to persevere.

The ABF Heart-Screening program seemed to be dying! We were not getting the attendance we received in the early years. There didn't seem to be urgency in the school districts or with the parents of young athletes. In early years from 2001 through 2011, the average attendance for the school screenings was 186. Screening attendance was a vital way to build funds needed for ABF operations. By the end of 2016, the average attendance had dropped to less than 130, and we were doing more heart-screening events that required more people-power. Even though volunteers don't cost hard dollars, feeding the volunteers, and delivering equipment to each event cost money. It seemed as if families had other priorities. Heart health wasn't on top of the list.

We had to scale back to save the program and save the heart-screening movement.

What is a young life REALLY worth?

Daily more than thirty children suffer a Sudden Cardiac Arrest in this country – most of those have no symptoms, and many of these children die[4].

Every three days, a young life lost due to Sudden Cardiac Arrest[5] just happens to be a high-school athlete … making the news, under-reporting the tragedy of the children lost to preventable Sudden Cardiac Arrest.

Too many children are dying, and there is a better way to prevent these deaths.

Educating the people; educating the medical industry:

At each step, there were more people to teach. In the early years, parents didn't believe that a child could die from playing sports. In the first years, there were many parents within Parent Heart Watch, which helped curb the tide and slow the death rates. Social media helped to bring awareness and education to the masses. The more parents sharing their children's stories on the airwaves, the sooner schools saw the value of placing Automatic External Defibrillators (AEDs).

The hurdle of using the AEDs in the schools as a gateway to fundraise for AED purchases made it easier to "screen more hearts and save more lives." Education of the masses is the key to changing

---

[4]   Strategies to Improve Cardiac Arrest Survival: A Time to Act, Robert Graham, Margaret A. McCoy, and Andrea M. Schultz, Institute of Medicine of the National Academies, ISBN 978-0-309-37199-5 | DOI 10.17226/21723, June 2015

[5]   "Sudden Cardiac Death in the Athlete," Authors: Mark S. Link, MD, N.A.; Mark Estes III, MD; 2012, American Heart Association

the mindsets that are firm in their beliefs. Many people, companies, and medical professionals still refuse to agree with all the factual data, that's been around for decades, regarding the value and benefits of heart-screenings.

Initially, I would avoid the people who had contrary, inaccurate views. As the years progressed, I knew it was time to take a stand and help re-educate as many people as possible.

There is also a considerable challenge regarding health care in lower-socio-economic communities to health care in general. These communities do not have the means to travel to our ABF fee-based heart-screening events. When we have hosted free heart-screening events in the lower-socio-economic neighborhoods, we experience low turnout. If an adverse finding were discovered in a child, where would the parents take him or her? How would they get the funds to care for a child with heart disease?

Regarding ABF Heart-Screenings in lower-socio-economic communities, the negative findings are almost triple than in the other more affluent areas. That sheds light on the real healthcare gap in our country. Access to adequate medical care, healthy foods, fundamental diet, and exercise programs don't often exist, which exacerbates the problems surrounding Sudden Cardiac Arrest. All these factors continue to weigh on my mind as we enter our 20th year and 3rd decade of hosting ABF Heart-Screening events. I choose to keep going and find new ways to help as many people as possible!

CHAPTER THIRTY-ONE

Making Our Way Globally

In 2006, our ABF Heart-Screening events were beginning to grow, and I needed more cardiology support. I had read an American Heart Association (AHA) paper regarding screenings performed in Italy. One of the authors was Dr. Antonio Pelliccia. I emailed him a request for help to connect me to other U.S. doctors. He replied within twenty-four hours that as a "scientist," he did not know what he could do. I responded, "I'll be in Rome on these dates, what works

Bridget, Brenda, Mary and Sharon in Rome, 2006

for you?" I invited my sister and ABF Board member, Brenda Laramore, to join me on this trip. Before traveling to Rome, I extended an invitation to meet in Italy with two other European mothers, Mary Vasseghi and Bridget Macallen, who had lost sons to HCM. After the start of Parent Heart Watch, our "Mom's Team" became popular in other countries that also lost children to hidden heart ailments. These two mothers shared my purpose and passion for helping save more children's lives from SCD. Children were dying all over the globe, and I needed to help wherever I could.

Mary, Dr. Antonio Pelliccia, Bridget and Sharon, 2006, Rome, Italy

Brenda, Mary, Bridget, and I enjoyed a nice dinner in Rome before our next day's meeting with Dr. Pelliccia. The next morning came early, and we made our way to the train station to get to our afternoon meeting at the Italian Institute of Sports Medicine outside of Rome. After several train transfers, we found our way to the facility. However, to our surprise, Dr. Pelliccia had been detained in another meeting with his superior. The receptionist invited us to get a coffee and snack in the cafeteria and wait for our meeting. The cafeteria windows looked out to the multitudes of young men participating in soccer drills. As we were sipping our beverages, Mary looked around and remarked, "Sharon, do you know what is so wonderful about this place?" I wasn't sure where she was going with her question, so I just shrugged. She continued, "All these children have had their hearts tested and are healthy to play sports!" The realization at that moment hit me like a tidal wave. We need "healthy heart certification" in the U.S. We need to protect ALL the children. I didn't want to get emotional, but that was so profound I couldn't help but tear up as that message touched my heart. Heart-safe children "at play" is the goal I have for my country.

Shortly after our snack-time, the receptionist escorted us to a meeting room to visit with Dr. Pelliccia. We made our introductions, and he was a gracious host, complimenting us on all the great work we were doing in our home countries. He was impressed with our ABF statistical screening numbers. They matched the findings in Italy. In 1984, Italy passed a law to screen all their athletes up to age thirty-five. Through heart-screenings, the Italians had reduced the death rate by eighty-nine percent. He shared a few names of U.S. doctors interested in heart-screenings. They included Dr. Jonathan Drezner, University of Washington, and several others, including doctors at Stanford University. Unfortunately, according to Dr. Pelliccia, many U.S. doctors had not accepted the Italian findings. It seems modern medicine has its roadblocks and politics.

I came back home energized to continue the fight. Parent Heart Watch (PHW) was new, and the leadership roles were taxing my efforts to build a significant heart-screening effort in the U.S. From the beginning, PHW was a colossal undertaking. Many of the parents who helped launch the group had no experience of "running a grassroots movement." Many were grappling with their grief, and underlying trauma of dealing with a young life snuffed out way too early because of Sudden Cardiac Arrest. I was still pretty raw on my own "grief journey" and it was a very stressful time for me. I had encounters with our PHW team that I regret. We all came from different backgrounds, careers, and education, with one thing in common, the loss of a child, each having our different way of dealing with the seemingly "unbearable." We kept persevering with our pain while grappling with our efforts to help the growing number of other parents who had lost children. With every step, we took massive action to protect children from future, preventable Sudden Cardiac Arrest. But, the process of pushing the boulder of change in our country was arduous and seemingly impossible.

The second version of the ABF Training Program was self-published in 2008 and the third version in 2014. The training program included a DVD with an inspirational video to create the team members to develop the screening and images of the heart-screening events in action. Also, the ABF Training Program included a CD with all the digital documents, and a more comprehensive 150-page binder full of details.

PHW taught me a lot about AEDs in schools. That seemed a way to grab the attention of the schools to host ABF Heart-Screening events and give them a fundraising model to obtain these life-saving devices. Not all schools had Automatic External Defibrillators (AEDs), and many were even resisting that life-saving equipment for fear of legal ramifications. Over time, the AED became a "standard of care" for schools, and the school districts were eager to find funding sources. Many Arizona school districts had the life saving equipment in their high schools but not in their elementary schools. As I also learned from PHW, children of all ages, genders, and races were dying from Sudden Cardiac Arrest. This was happening both on the playground and during sports activities. As well, the staff of both elementary and high schools were at risk of Sudden Cardiac Arrest. The "Heart-Screenings for AEDs" program was booming for the first ten years.

By 2010, the economic downturn had slowed the effort of all fundraising and particularly heart-screening attendance. The rebound of the economy occurred by the end of 2014, which allowed me to retire from my contractor/computer programming job. I was now able to concentrate full time on support of the ABF Trained Teams, hosting ABF Heart-Screening events, and placing AEDs.

Starting in June of 2015, summer interns flowed through the ABF doors to start digitizing our database. Volunteers are the heart-blood of ABF. Utilizing young students eager to learn about our program became the magic to share our curriculum with our country's future leaders. The purpose of digitizing the paper was to make the screening results more transparent and professional for research. We completed digitizing the screening paperwork by the summer of 2019.

CHAPTER THIRTY-TWO

Screening in Colorado for Anthony's Half-sister

Starting in 2005, I looked to other states across the country to host screenings and keep ABF afloat. By 2009, we did our first Colorado screening. I chose to do a Colorado screening to support Anthony's other family. Living in Colorado Springs were his two half-sisters, Megan, Dani, and half-brother, Bobby. Anthony never got a chance to meet his siblings. However, several times over the years, I had sent materials to the family through Anthony's biological father, Joe, with information about HCM and the importance of screening the family. Subsequently, in late 2008 Anthony's younger half-sister, Dani, contacted me through our ABF website. At the time she believed she might have the same thing Anthony had, due to similar symptoms and family history. She was sixteen years old, and Dani posted a message to me asking, "Are there organizations in Colorado that do screenings?" At that time, I knew of none.

Through several follow-up conversations with Dani's mother, Pati, I learned that Joe had never shared with his wife and children the material about heart health and heart-screenings I had sent him several times in the past. She was astounded to learn that HCM was genetic, and her children were at risk of Sudden Cardiac Death.

They were not married much longer, not because of what I had sent, but what seemed to be his unresolved issues with grief. I divorced Anthony's father, Joe, in 1980, when Anthony was just one, and Joe chose not to be a 'weekend father.' Within a year of our divorce, Joe opposed the divorce decree regarding the child support payment of a very reasonable $100 a month and left the state. He abandoned us to start a different life. We had to fend for ourselves.

In 1994, after Allen and I divorced, my younger sister, Teresa, encouraged Joe to reach out to us. She explained to him, without my permission, "Anthony needed a father in his life," I'm not sure what moved him to reach out then, but Anthony didn't want anything to do with meeting him when he did. I encouraged Anthony to reconnect, not just for his well-being, but also to get to know his siblings. Anthony was technically an only child. Allen had his son, Chris, from a previous marriage, and Anthony had a relationship with his stepbrother over the last three years Allen and I were married. However, Anthony had never met his half-siblings, and sadly, his death closed the door to that opportunity. My explanation to Anthony went something like this, "What if you need a kidney someday? Those kids might be a match."

The half-truth to that statement was that they needed to know their own risk of this genetic heart condition that didn't seem to have a source. Still to this day, no one in our family had or has this condition, other than Anthony. Also, no one on his biological father's side of the family seemed to have the disease.

Therefore, in 2009, I agreed to come to Colorado and start the search for resources to screen in Colorado Springs. We had a few ultrasound techs willing to support the program. Also, we found a doctor who would help us. My ultrasound technician friend, Eleanor Glass, agreed to travel with me from Arizona to Colorado.

We donated two Automatic External Defibrillators (AEDs) to schools in the area; Lewis-Palmer High School, the host screening school, and one to Dani's high school, Manitou Springs High School. The day in March of the screening event, we screened eighty-two people. We found six problems, and one "Possible Life-Threatening" issue. All of Anthony's half-siblings and stepmother volunteered at the event. ABF hosted a small heart-screening event; ABF shared the best gift of all, *'Peace of Mind,'* with most attendees.

It was not easy to interact with my ex-husband, Joe, Anthony's biological father. Later, I found out that he played the "woe is me" card to the registration team and the people administering his screening tests. He shared "his agony" with the group that his son died, and we all needed to feel sorry for him. It made me angry as this man abandoned our son. He wanted sympathy from the heart-screening team. I steemed with anger when I spoke to him the next month.

He called wanting more sympathy from me, and I let him have it with both barrels. How could he want others to feel so sorry for him and not have the decency to pay Anthony's child support and then, years later, withhold the "heart-health" information about HCM from the mother of his other children? I was appalled, disturbed, and told him never to call me again. I learned another lesson. If I were to speak with anyone in that family, it would be his other children's mother, not him.

I screened in Colorado yearly, from 2014 up to events we plan to offer as soon as our leaders decide to row their oars in the same direction and defeat the COVID-19 pandemic. After 2020, we intend to host future events in Denver communities. It always made sense for me to dovetail a Kansas event with a Colorado event. I would drive through parts of Colorado during the trek from Kansas to Arizona. Colorado is somewhat on the way in either direction.

By 2017, we had made some good progress in the Colorado schools with the help of the SCAA Denver Chapter led by Mary Tappe and with the help of Bob and Troy Bowman. In 2008, I invited Bob Bowman to attend the Parent Heart Watch (PHW) meeting in Seattle. At the time, Bob and Troy were still living in Montana after the sudden death of their son, Jeffrey, in August 2007. Jeffrey had suffered a Sudden Cardiac Arrest during his first football workout, and the school's AED was locked up and unavailable to rescue him. The Bowman family became staunch advocates for Automatic External

Defibrillator (AED) placement and CPR training with their foundation, the Jeffrey Bowman Heart Fund. Their support to advocate for screening events was an excellent match for ABF.

Therefore, in 2017, I was able to host a small event in Aurora, Colorado. Troy Bowman connected ABF to the school district in Aurora, Colorado. The Aurora School District needed additional AEDs, and "Heart-Screenings for AEDs" seemed a good match. The community was not in an affluent area, and the attendance was low, with fewer than 100 people. However, with the Jeffrey Bowman Heart Fund's help, the school district was gifted two AEDs.

My bubbly friend, Shirley Serrault, made the drive with me from the Kansas State University ABF Heart-Screening event more adventuresome. We made an overnight stop in Kearny, Nebraska, on our way to Aurora. Lindsay, Shirley's granddaughter, caravanned down to the Denver area with us to help at the Aurora School District heart-screening event.

On the first day in Aurora, we visited the school district office and checked out the Saturday event facility. We were met by Troy Bowman and mapped out the set-up for the next day's screening event. After our meeting, we were due some sustenance and checked out the local establishments on my Smartphone. There were many restaurants to choose from, so we selected one on a whim. Of course, I was pulling a trailer behind my vehicle, and my parking skills or lack thereof made me park in several spots on a diagonal not too far from the restaurant. That got the attention of another incoming patron of the establishment.

When my friends and I departed my truck, we started to walk toward the restaurant. I thought I heard someone shout my name, but we were all together, so I was unsure of the commotion source. Then I heard my name again, but this time it was my maiden name, Sharon Foote. I turned to see two women approaching us rather hurriedly. One of the women shouted my name again, and I responded, "Yes." I didn't recognize the two women that were approaching our group. She told me, "It's Karen Kinser!" I was shocked to run into my college friend from Friends University in Wichita, Kansas, in a Colorado parking lot. We made introductions to the group and enjoyed a meal together. Since that connection, we exchanged our latest email address and became friends on Facebook to ensure our continued camaraderie. Three degrees of separation! Is it the Anthony Bates Foundation or Facebook? You decide!

We hosted multiple events in Colorado with the Douglas County School District, which worked out well for several years. With the help of the Sudden Cardiac Arrest Association (SCAA) Denver Chapter, I was able to tap into their volunteer force and make better connections in the medical industry. The world sometimes turns in different ways and allows old relationships to become new again (remember the story of "Sharon and Will.")

Early in our ABF Heart-Screening program and Automatic External Defibrillator placement, Ed Walsh came into my life. Ed was at the first Parent Heart Watch (PHW) meeting in Las Vegas. We worked together in placing AEDs. Ed and his son, Sean, were great in educating me about AED's. I learned a lot from those two men regarding the ins-and-outs of the technology. Ed and Sean got out of the AED business after a bad partnership with their AED distributor. Not everyone has good intentions in this business of "saving young lives!" I get it that businesses need to make a profit, but sacrificing people and their livelihood does not make for the best business strategy. Life does not come with a handbook, life is too short, and life is too valuable. Doing the right thing goes a long way!

What I did not know about Ed was that he had heart disease. In September 2018, he had a Sudden Cardiac Arrest in a Colorado park while watching his granddaughter play soccer. His cardiac nurse daughter, Kara Baker, performed CPR on Ed for twenty minutes, but Ed died before the EMTs arrived. There was no AED available to save Ed's life. I was heartbroken for Ed's family.

Right after Ed died, Kara reached out to me. The family wanted to send donations to ABF instead of flowers at her father's funeral. Ed's sudden loss affected me very deeply. I wanted to do more in Ed's memory. It turns out that within the Douglas County School District is where Kara and her family live. After speaking with Kara, we agreed to host a Highlands Ranch screening in honor of her father and my friend, Ed. In honor of Ed, we have screened there for several years and are raising funds to place AED's in Colorado's parks. We had to postpone the 2020 Spring ABF Heart-Screening event due to the

COVID-19 pandemic, but we will persevere and reschedule when safety returns to our communities.

The sad truth for all non-profits is when the money runs out, so do the programs and their services. Good stewardship is necessary for all non-profits due to the cyclical environment of giving. How can non-profit organizations reach sustainability without ongoing donations from the public, family, and friends of those screened and those saved? At these lean times, passion, perseverance and proper planning within an organization drive the mission's efforts.

As you can see throughout my book, challenges exist running a Non-Profit Organization (NPO). The Parent Heart Watch (PHW) family, who created the Jeffrey Bowman Heart Fund, closed its doors in 2018. They ran their NPO for ten years after the death of their child. By the time, they hit that milestone, the tides of time and life had turned against them and gotten in the way. The message sent out to their community of supporters read they felt it was time to close their NPO. Challenges NPO's face are real; connecting to our audience of young people, health challenges of aging leaders; non-stop fundraising to keep the lights on; working other jobs to pay bills. These are all issues faced by NPOs.

Meanwhile, to provide NPO's program services to the community, we stretch funds thin. As in ABF, for every dollar donated we return $1.58 of services to the communities we serve. That is an example of stretching every penny! Other NPOs have faded away during these past twenty years of ABF's existence. However, some NPO's have stayed strong and brought in substantial donations and gifts to continue to provide services to their communities.

I hope that this book's stories regarding several of the children we have saved inspire more funding sources to support nationwide screenings in both large cities and small rural towns. All children, regardless of socio-economic background, deserve to live a full life to adulthood and the later golden years. ABF has pursued that goal over the past two decades and continues to champion our goals and programs into the next. Every child's life is precious! All children deserve a full life to adulthood and later golden years. ABF has been striving to make that happen for children everywhere!

CHAPTER THIRTY-THREE

Presenting My 'New' Self to the World!

The trauma of my childhood and the self-image issues I carried through my marriages and divorces left me a much-damaged young adult. I stepped into the role of a young mother with determination and courage. I was not going to make the same mistakes as my mother; I would be there as a guide and a consistent source of love for my child. I still had many abandonment issues to carry around, though, so I tried to release the anxieties and frustrations. I exercised a lot when I was in my thirties. By the time Anthony died, I had stopped going to the gym; I had stopped caring about myself and was unwilling to look inward for a long time.

Unity of Phoenix Chaplain Program allowed me to examine the hardened surface of my heart. I was able to break open some of the shell of sadness that I carried around and release and let go the pain. During my "grief journey," I was looking for that magic milestone. Five years, ten years, fifteen years there was no magic eraser for this "grief" I carried. When would I be cured of the "years of misery" we call "grief?" It turns out we carry our "grief" for the rest of our life on this Earth plane. I had to learn to live with it, alongside it, and not "in" it, dragging me down. The Unity of Phoenix Chaplain Program taught me much of this principle to go within and be in the magic of knowing.

When Will came into my life, he began to guide me, and he brought out the softer side of "Sharon." He is gentle, calm, confident, patient, and persistent in his approach, although initially, I resisted his guidance. Occasionally, Will reminds me that I am stubborn. He has encouraged me to make some significant lifestyle changes. We had been going to the gym together, and we have created a home gym during the COVID-19 pandemic. He has encouraged me to eat right and take care of myself by meditating and getting enough sleep. I still work too much, but I am functioning more efficiently and have a renewed commitment to children's "heart-health" here and worldwide. That is what passion looks like to me.

I can't bring my son, Anthony, back, but I intend to save as many young people as possible as we stay viable as an NPO. I plan to make a difference in our world! I continue to stand up for the truth about heart disease in children and preventable Sudden Cardiac Death with proper screening. If the Institute of Medicine (IOM)[6] estimates are accurate, over 12,000 youth suffer from Sudden Cardiac Arrest (SCA) each year, meaning well **over a quarter of a million children have experienced an SCA since Anthony died.** That turns into 500,000 grieving parents who have had to experience the same depth and breadth of my grief. According to the American Heart Association (AHA), only 8% of people who suffer an out-of-hospital SCA will survive. That translates to just 20,000 children who might have survived SCA since 2000. We have to do better! *Our future and the future of our nation depend on saving these children!*

Take a stand with me and take the Parent Heart Watch (PHW) pledge, "Eliminate preventable Sudden Cardiac Arrest in young children by 2030!"

"Screen 'Em ALL" #GotHeartGetScreened

"Make a difference in Your Community!" I will do my part to continue the effort and persevere for our country's children and families!

---

[6]   Strategies to Improve Cardiac Arrest Survival: A Time to Act, Robert Graham, Margaret A. McCoy, and Andrea M. Schultz, Institute of Medicine of the National Academies, ISBN 978-0-309-37199-5 | DOI 10.17226/21723, June 2015

CHAPTER THIRTY-FOUR

Anthony's "Second Death" at K-State

July 31, 2020, marked twenty years since Anthony died. For the first eighteen years, ABF screened Kansas State University athletes. Coach Bill Snyder was our connection until his two retirements. To help Kansas State University remain heart-safe, we endured many bumps in our "partnership" road. Coach Snyder retired the first time in 2006. When Coach Ron Prince took over, the relationship was not so inviting. Coach Prince didn't connect with my son, and all he cared about was his current football players. His community connections were limited. He didn't want ABF to screen the other K-State athletes, and he did not wish for the ABF Heart-Screening event to open up to the public. By 2008, Coach Prince cut off our public screening program, and we only screened fifty-one people that year, mostly football players. Coach Prince's lack of concern for his community crushed me.

From 2006 to the end of 2008, Coach Prince didn't treat me like "Kansas State Family." THE BIG QUESTION IS WHY? Even though I asked for meetings, he never met with me when I would visit the school to provide screenings to his football players. I was hurt and disturbed by his demeanor. Many other people in Manhattan, Kansas, shared my feelings. KSU bought out his contract in a legal battle and subsequently pushed out Coach Prince. By the 2009 football and ABF Heart-Screening event season, Coach Snyder was back at the helm, and we hosted large heart-screening events at Kansas State University for nine more years.

In all the years I hosted ABF Heart-Screening events at Kansas State, my efforts taught me a lot about the other Division I schools hosting other heart-screening events. I discovered the University of Georgia (UofG) had provided heart-screens to their athletes for nearly a decade before Anthony's death. It seemed that some people took heed to the 1996 American Heart Association (AHA) report that stated, "Some kind of cardiac evaluation should be done for the athletes." I first met the UofG Athletic Trainer, Ron Courson, in early February 2006 during the first "Prevention of Sudden Cardiac Death in Athletes" conference in Jackson, Mississippi. That was the conference delayed by Hurricane Katrina. The one I navigated through an ice storm to attend.

From the 2005 ESPN's "Outside the Lines" program, I learned University of Georgia (UofG) was screening their athletes and paying technicians to administer the tests and cardiologists to read the results, at a total of $137 per player. The episode highlighted the ABF screening program. In my discoveries, I learned that not all NCAA athletic programs are equal. These facts and details made my head swim, and emotions boil with anger. All athletes sacrifice so much of their own young lives for their sport, but not all university sports programs sacrifice to provide athletes these life-saving heart tests. An ECG/EKG test costs less than $25 during a mass-screening event. When these heart tests are provided in more significant quantities, the costs are less than $5 each. Why can't we do the bare minimum to protect the youth of this nation?

When I first started ABF Heart-Screening events for Kansas State University Athletic Department, Coach Snyder would give ABF the proceeds from the KSU Football Team Spring games. He would split the funds between the Anthony Bates Memorial Fund and the KSU Library Fund. As long as the weather was good, there would be a few thousand dollars to give to each group. Through additional fund-raising, golf-tournaments, even raffles, and solicitation of corporate donations, ABF could survive.

Due to "compliance" issues, Coach Snyder told me he was limited in his budget to offer outside groups the funds from the "KSU Football Team Spring games." His athletic budget was strict, and the rulebooks (compliance guidelines) were thick and comprehensive. He explained that he couldn't spend the university's football budget on the "unsanctioned" heart-screenings for the athletes. During the ABF Heart-Screening events at KSU, **the NCAA did not require and still does not require heart tests or heart screens for the athletes that contribute to their profits.** In my opinion, the NCAA's lack of mandatory testing is a travesty that makes the NCAA culpable <u>every time</u> a young athlete dies from an undiagnosed heart condition. The NCAA could prevent these deaths through proper heart-screening tests. Group screening would <u>cost less than $25 per person</u>, the cost of the heart-screening by Anthony Bates Foundation, and many heart-screening organizations, including ABF Trained Teams across the U.S.

In 2002, the "spring game" receipts from Kansas State University Football were to screen approximately 200 athletes in the fall. The funds ABF received were a little over $800. That came out to be about <u>twenty-five cents per athlete</u>. I flew back and forth from Arizona to Kansas, but I also had to ship supplies and equipment. Luckily, I was spared the added hotel expenses through the generosity of my Kansas "Purple People" friends who let me stay in their homes. That year was a huge wake-up call for me, especially when the school announced the initial plans for renovations to the football complex and athletic facility. This multi-million dollar project would create better venues and more seats. I thought, *"How about investing a small amount of money, in comparison, and save some young lives?"*

My son was dead, and I carried a vow in my heart to protect and prevent other athletes from experiencing the same fate. I was moving Anthony's legacy forward to prevent other families from feeling what I felt every day; the unbearable pain, loss, devastation. I just wanted to prevent more unnecessary deaths. However, Kansas State University Athletic Department chose to give ABF only $800 while spending millions to appease their alumni and build more seats for paying spectators. I was unequivocally pissed off!

I struggled on for a few more years. We had fundraisers and did other campaigns to make up the difference. Then in 2005, ESPN's "Outside the Lines" did a piece on the Anthony Bates Foundation. Initially, the reporter, Steve Delson, explained to me the article was supposed to be a "warm and fuzzy" report. It would outline a "mother on a mission" to save other athletes from the same fate as my son, Anthony. However, during our taping of the ABF Heart-Screening event at Anthony's high school, Mountain Pointe, there was a Sudden Cardiac Death of an athlete at the University of Arizona (UofA). The event of his death shifted the emphasis of the story.

There was a flurry of script changes for Steve Delson, ESPN Reporter. He went to University of Arizona (UofA) in Tucson, Arizona to interview the athletic department and team doctor. In the fall of 2005, McCollins Umeh had died six hours after walking onto the UofA campus. Instead, that date, which should have been marked with excitement and euphoria, for McCollins Umeh, became etched on a head stone. McCollins had a team sports physical, went to a football meeting, had lunch, and went to football practice, and there experienced a Sudden Cardiac Arrest. He was rushed to the hospital and subsequently died.

The part of the interview about McCollin Umeh's death that was additionally gut-wrenching, to me, was when ESPN uncovered the University of Georgia (UofG) screening program of $137 per athlete. That same year our support from Kansas State University was an abysmal less than ten dollars per athlete! It was like throwing salt onto my deep wounds. The devastating pain of Anthony's loss instantly returned to my heart and soul. After screening at KSU for five years, their atrocious, cavalier, lack of regard for our services to their athletes and community was appalling. ABF was undoubtedly worth the same compensation as the program at the UofG. Something had to change!

The program aired the day I was in Kansas at the KSU Alumni Center, hosting that year's ABF Heart-Screening event. Even in pain, after discovering discrepancies around compensation issues, I had to put on an event. Volunteers and athletes were waiting for us to provide excellent service, which we always did! Each time I was in Kansas, ABF provided value to the athletes who showed up to get their heart screened and others in the general public who desired to know their heart health or that of their child.

When I returned home to Arizona, I made VHS copies (it was before DVDs and digital capture) of the program. I sent one to the Athletic Director of KSU, Tim Weiser (A.D. from 2001 – 2008), one to Coach Bill Snyder, and one to the newly promoted head athletic trainer of KSU, Matt Thomason. I had to stand up for myself, for ABF, and the people of Manhattan, Kansas. The university was a multi-million dollar operation taking advantage of a grieving mother and additionally undervaluing heart-screenings designed to protect their athletes. Where were KSU's priorities?

My note enclosed with the videotape to Tim Weiser was blunt, "I'm bleeding here, and I need your help." During my spring trip to Kansas the next year in 2006, head athletic trainer, Matt Thomason set up a breakfast meeting with the Athletic Director, Tim Weiser. Matt was on my side and enthusiastic about continuing the ABF Heart-Screening events for the athletes at KSU. I shared my numbers and my concern about the need for support from the university. Mr. Weiser committed to $5,000 from the athletic department budget to host screenings for the players and continue to keep them open to the public.

That was approximately $25 per player, with an average of 200 athletes attending the ABF Heart-Screening event. The new sponsorship from Kansas State University Athletic Department would allow the ABF Heart-Screening events to continue. Additionally, a small donation request would allow KSU students, staff, and members of the public to receive heart-screening tests. An average of fifty people from the community came to the Kansas State University ABF Heart-Screening events. The donations from the public would bring in a few hundred dollars. Every dollar helped keep ABF operational.

That agreement continued for about four years (2006 to 2010) until the university had a significant controversy. Do you remember that KSU "compliance" department I referred to earlier? Somehow, in 2009 amid the time Coach Prince left the helm, the Kansas Board of Regents administered a regular audit, which discovered some funds inappropriately used for members inside the athletic department. I don't have all the details, but several members of the KSU Athletic Department were either fired or forced to retired.

I received a phone call from the internal auditor of Kansas State University. The auditor asked me about the funds paid to the Anthony Bates Foundation (ABF). That year two $5,000 checks had been issued from the Kansas State University Athletic Department funds to ABF. But we only received one check for $5,000. The auditor thanked me for my time, and I didn't hear from him again. I did find out from my friend, Shirley Serrault, that the local newspaper ran a story about several people at KSU losing their jobs over this scandal. It was a sad time for KSU.

Before the 2009 Coach Prince debacle, the Athletic Director, Tim Weiser, got a promotion to the Big 12 as the Deputy Commissioner. Also, the University President, Jon Wefald, was forced to retire. The next year our sponsorship increased to $10,000. I never questioned the reason for the increase. However, even the addition of that amount of money underfunded ABF screenings to only $50 per player. The additional sponsorship from KSU was not $137 or $185 per player, which was what the current increased market price. ABF was getting ripped off!

For the next six years, additional Kansas State University Athletic Department-funded construction projects occurred at a multi-million dollar level. We continued, for this duration of time, until I decided to question the sponsorship. Gene Taylor took over as the new Athletic Director (2017 to present), and I requested a meeting. The sponsorship was not covering our costs. More and more universities provide screenings to their athletes and pay the near-market price of $75 per athlete. Why did ABF have to get inferior treatment when we were the trailblazers in screening athletes?

We agreed upon an increase in the Kansas State University Athletic Department sponsorship of ABF Heart-Screenings to an annual amount of $15,000. However, the number of athletes increased from 150 to nearly 250 people in a screening. Besides, with the extra athletes to screen, we were burning out our volunteers. By 2017, the local hospital stopped sending ultrasound technicians to our event, as they claimed their techs as overworked even in the hospital. Keep in mind; the hospital had to pay the technicians' overtime if they attended our event. The hospital claimed the screening cost them over $20,000 each year, even though the cardiologists were independent of the hospital. I am confident they factored the value of the echocardiogram equipment and both the technicians and the doctors' time. By the middle of 2015, we knew that small-town hospitals were on tight budgets. These kinds of issues are real. There are challenges when a community event relies on support from the small local hospital. Not everyone can help every time. Not all hospitals are the same.

During the 2014 annual Heart-2-Heart Parent Heart Watch Conference, screening organizations such as ABF learned of new technology. The CardeaScreen Electrocardiogram (ECG/EKG) machines, designed and manufactured by Dave Hadley, PhD., contained the "Seattle Criteria" algorithms, which picked up arrhythmias (abnormal rhythms) in children that could potentially cause Sudden Cardiac Death. In late 2012 they published a paper, *"Electrocardiographic interpretation in athletes; the 'Seattle Criteria.'"* The authors included Dr. Jonathan Drezner and twenty renowned cardiologists, including Dr. Vicki Vetter, and electrophysiologists (heart rhythm doctors.) This paper and ECG standards were relevant in the creation of CardeaScreen by Dr. Hadley.

By the end of 2014, ABF had funds raised and future events planned from heart-screening events to purchase eight CardeaScreen Electrocardiogram (ECG/EKG) systems with printers for our upcoming heart-screening events. My college-age nephew, Chase Decker, came to Phoenix over his Christmas break to help set up the equipment. We had quite a learning curve, but we managed with Dr. Dave Hadley and his team. Using CardeaScreen systems in the ABF Heart-Screening events, the screening data would be more appealing for research. Research with ABF data seemed to be long overdue. ECG/EKG (electrical studies of the heart rhythm) screening tests were only one part of our screening protocol. ABF uses ultrasound (images of the heart function and measurements of the heart walls) in our heart-screening protocol to validate the ECG screening tests to eliminate false positives and prove "athlete's heart" (a concentric enlargement of the heart) compared to "HCM" (an abnormally shaped enlarged heart.)

Due to this new equipment, our shipping costs were skyrocketing. The fact of the matter is that to become more efficient in the screening process, ABF needed to own more of our equipment. However, the more equipment we owned, the costlier it was to ship, due to the extra weight. Our operating costs were increasing every year, and our funds did not meet the program's expenses. ABF had to work, think, and function as a business to be sustainable. We had to analyze our income, losses, and be strategic in negotiating all our events. The key to the survival of any non-profit is keeping overhead low and fundraising to match and exceed the program levels. Additionally, plans for growth with new funds are necessary regarding equipment desires and increased people's power.

Besides, during the 2016 KSU ABF Heart-Screening event, we maxed out the community volunteer cardiologists. Two community cardiologists confirmed their attendance before our Heart-Screening event but did not show up. Without local cardiology and community support, the screening program was dying like the athletes who had HCM but went undiagnosed because they never received a heart-screen.

After we hosted the 2016 heart-screening event, I took the 278 paper results into Coach Bill Snyder's office. I told him how disappointed I was with the politics played by the community hospital, medical professionals, and technicians. I asked him to use his community influence to reach out to the doctors and review the results after the event. In our Arizona Heart-Screening events, ABF had already changed our protocol to match the demand of cardiologists. Doctors are too busy to sit with us for six to eight hours on a Saturday and individually review the results with the attendees.

Coach Snyder had his head athletic trainer, Matt Thomason, reach out to the team doctor, Keith Wright, at Stonecreek Family Medicine. Three area cardiologists "agreed" to split the paper stack into three equal piles and review the results. Our primary resource and long-time supporter, Dr. James Hurtig, had the results back to Matt within a month. Dr. Hurtig had cared for Anthony on the day he died. His support and generosity of his time were paramount. Most cardiologists' time are stretched between availability for community support, regular patient care, cardiac emergencies, and home life.

We know their demands are high in our country and we have always been respectful of our volunteer cardiologists' time.

The other two doctors were not as supportive about reading the results after the event. There is still a stigma in the screening effort by doctors. If the doctors do not see the patients directly, there are fears concerning liability. Screening programs are not the same as diagnostic tests. Screenings are preventive medicine to give people with the standard result peace of mind. Even still within our country and the medical community, prevention of disease is not a priority. On average, just ten percent of people screened will need further evaluation. Proper medical professionals will then follow-up with these young people and athletes for additional testing and review.

Dr. R., one of the two doctors with remaining unread studies, had the second pile of results from September until January. Mainly, Matt was waiting for all three doctors to finish their review before sending the results back to ABF. When I received the results from Matt Thomason, Dr. R. had an excessive amount of abnormal findings, more than thirty percent. Keep in mind, the average abnormal results at any given ABF Heart-Screening event is around ten percent. This red flag pushed me to have these results reviewed by two separate doctors, one in Phoenix and the other from Stanford University, referred to me by Dr. Dave Hadley of CardeaScreen. After the double-blind study, the screening results were much lower, at five percent.

Then the third doctor, Dr. K., refused to review any of the screening results. He felt his liability was too high. He had not witnessed the actual screening event. Matt Thomason conveyed to me; the third doctor did not feel comfortable reviewing the results outside the heart-screening event. Keep in mind; this doctor had participated in a previous screening and had confirmed he would participate that year but didn't show up, call, or let ABF know he wouldn't be available. That is just rude. I have gotten increasingly more of that type of "doctor" behavior over the years.

I was able to have the third pile of KSU ABF Heart-Screening results reviewed in January, four months after the event. The excessive delay of all test results was not acceptable. If we couldn't rely on Kansas doctors, who could we rely on for support with rural heart-screening events? Once again, our Phoenix cardiologists, Doctors Ed Rhee,

Robert Puntel, and Jeff Pakula came through for ABF. I would like to recognize the many years of support from these doctors. Since 2004, Dr. Jeff Pakula and I have been working together since I shared the first video production of the ABF "What is HCM?" By 2006, I met Dr. Ed Rhee at St. Joseph Hospital during his Grand Rounds talk on "Sudden Cardiac Arrest in the Young." After his presentation, Dr. Stephen Pophal introduced him to me, and I shared the current statistics of the ABF Heart-Screening data. Dr. Ed Rhee now works at Phoenix Children's Hospital (PCH) and supports the ABF Heart-Screening Program. By 2008, Dr. Robert Puntel came to PCH via Seattle and instantly became a huge advocate and supporter of the ABF Heart-Screening Program. Several other doctors have come and gone during our twenty years of heart-screening events in Arizona and many parts of the country. These three doctors are true "Heart Champions" for young people!

By the end of the 2016 Kansas State University ABF Heart-Screening event debacle, I committed to changing our relationship with KSU! ABF did bill the Kansas State University Athletic Department for the extra 111 students sent to the screenings. The initial sponsorship was to cover 100 athletes. That year we screened 212 athletes. ABF charged KSU with an additional fee for the extra work needed to over-read two-thirds of the heart-screening results. By the end of our re-negotiation, the Kansas State University Athletic Department raised its sponsorship fee to $25,000 or $125 per athlete (still under market value.)

For a short time, there seemed to be light at the end of the tunnel. In October 2017, I finally contacted the right research personnel, Carl Ade, in the KSU research department. We started building a partnership with the Sports Medicine Department to analyze the multiple years of data within the ABF Heart-Screening Program. The researchers would focus on the heart studies of the Kansas State University athletes to include follow-up over several years.

In 2017, the Kansas State University Athletic Department purchased three CardeaScreen Electrocardiogram (ECG/EKG) systems. They attempted to hold their screenings without ABF. That was personally a "low blow." The "last straw" came when KSU Head Football Coach Bill Snyder retired for the second and final time, and ABF lost its most prominent advocate. Shortly after that, ABF became estranged from KSU. The research program we tried to set up with KSU could not be completed without ABF, as there was no more available data on KSU athletes. According to Matt Thomason, KSU was deleting the digital data after the athletic department printed a copy of the ECG for its paper record.

The reports from the other athletic teams were grim. In 2017, I contacted the various sports-teams within KSU Athletic Department; I discovered that KSU had not screened the athletes in the golf, rowing, track and field, and the soccer teams. I sent emails to the athletic director and all the athletic trainers inviting the unscreened athletes to our Kansas ABF Heart-Screening event in 2017. Unfortunately and painfully, our 2017 heart-screening event progressed without KSU athletes. No one replied to my message until a week before the event. I had to make phone calls and additional emails to get a reply for a message sent six weeks prior. I finally got the follow-up email from the Athletic Director, Gene Taylor, who told me that Matt Thomason confirmed, "Everyone has been and does get screened. So we will not be sending anyone to the Manhattan screening." I will be watching and praying they take care of their KSU athletes.

By the end of 2018, the research agreement fizzled. With no data available from the KSU athletes' screenings, the KSU Sports Medicine Department was no longer interested in pursuing a research agreement with ABF.

It was as if my son "died a second time." Kansas State University stopped inviting ABF to screen their athletes, and my "grief journey" seemed to backslide to the early years. These circumstances involving people with their agendas stifled a program producing results in helping to keep their athletes and community safe. Budget cuts were an excuse, but the reality was evident with millions of dollars spent on upgrading the stadium. In retrospect, I was naïve to think that I was part of the Kansas State Family. However, administrators often have "short memories," and new administrators had no memories of ABF, Anthony, or me.

When I started the heart-screening efforts with Kansas State University, I desired that the university eventually take on its heart-screening program. It just was so frustrating to have the research lined up, and then the screening cut off. Once again, I realize I cannot control people, budgets, or circumstances; my hope for KSU is that someday, heart-screenings and researchers would align their programs. It is a matter of life and death, which they have forgotten, by forgetting Anthony, his legacy, and what ABF did for their athletes and community.

Every day, another 891 people die from Sudden Cardiac Arrest in this country, and my heart bleeds for their families. I continue to ask the hard questions. Why are athletic programs in high schools, colleges, and universities overlooking heart-health and protection from Sudden Cardiac Arrest for their student-athletes? When will "screening young hearts and saving young lives" take precedence over bigger, flashier, new stadiums to feed investors and alumni egos? When will this insanity end?

CHAPTER THIRTY-FIVE

Challenges with the NCAA

Through the twenty years since Anthony's death I have faced many political roadblocks in youth sports, especially by large, influential organizations on the national level. Money talks and many worthy causes often get pushed to the back burner. In 1996, four years before Anthony's death, the American Heart Association (AHA) published a study on athletes that claimed, "Some kind of cardiac evaluation was necessary for young athletes, but the NCAA was exempt."[7] The only reason I could see for that exemption was to "save money." The power of the NCAA is monstrous and monopolistic. How could one large organization care so little about the well-being of their athletes? It came to light for me in another published paper in 2012, sixteen years after the 1996 paper and twelve years after Anthony's death, *the NCAA is responsible for the athletes they use and abuse!*

---

[7] "Cardiovascular Preparticipation Screening of Competitive Athletes" (*Circulation.* 1996;94:850–856), Authors: Barry J. Maron, Paul D. Thompson, James C. Puffer, Christopher A. McGrew, William B. Strong, Pamela S. Douglas, Luther T. Clark, Matthew J. Mitten, Michael H. Crawford, Dianne L. Atkins, David J. Driscoll, and Andrew E. Epstein.

This 2012 study done in Tel Aviv, Israel outlines the cost-burden to the NCAA of heart-screening that "only" would save a few lives, "A 20-year program of ECG screening of young competitive athletes in the United States would cost between $51 and $69 billion and could be expected to save 4,813 lives. Accordingly, the cost per life saved is likely to range between $10.6 and $14.4 million."[8]

Through all the disagreements I have endured, the toughest has been with the NCAA. I am genuinely disappointed that a money-making machine, such as the NCAA, couldn't find the funds, in their vast balance sheet and investment portfolio, to heart-screen athletes for the minimum of a $25 Electrocardiogram (ECG/EKG.) Young athletes continue to die, some on the field and others in their sleep. The NCAA's non-action stance on heart disease in young people is deplorable.

There is a life-insurance accidental-death policy that the NCAA purchases each year to cover every student-athlete with a "sudden death benefit." If the player dies during a "sanctioned" event, the life insurance company will pay that amount to the player's beneficiaries, parents, or family. Included in the coverage for the NCAA life insurance policy is a "cardiac" clause. If a student-athlete dies from a cardiac event, the insurance policy will pay a "sudden death benefit." This insurance policy and "cardiac" provision have been in effect since 1998. Two years before Anthony died!

I didn't know about this insurance policy until after Anthony died. Kansas State University and the NCAA never shared this insurance policy information with me. It was not until the University of Arizona (UofA) player, McCollins Umeh died, in 2005, that I found out about the KSU policy. After his death, I took a Tucson trip to invite UofA to host an ABF Heart-Screening event for their athletes. At that time, Mike Stoops was the head coach, formerly of Oklahoma University, by way of Kansas State University. I was sure I had an "in," because Erik Harper, another former KSU coach, was also coaching at UofA. Erik had been a coach at KSU when Anthony died and had participated in a few of the Anthony Bates Foundation

---

8   "Preventing Sudden Death of Athletes With Electrocardiographic Screening" (Journal of the American College of Cardiology, Vol. 60, No. 22, 2012), Authors: Amir Halkin, MD, Arie Steinvil, MD, Raphael Rosso, MD, Arnon Adler, MD, Uri Rozovski, MD, Sami Viskin, MD: Tel Aviv, Israel

golf tournaments in Kansas. I met with Erick and we talked about the sadness of McCollins Umeh's sudden death a few months prior. Subsequently, McCollins' tragic death was in that ESPN "Outside the Lines" program with ABF. Erik said to me, "At least the family will get a death benefit." I was puzzled, as I had never heard that term before. "Death benefit?" I asked him to explain. He was vague and somewhat embarrassed that I had not received any information about this "death benefit" from Anthony's death.

When I returned to my car, I immediately called the Kansas State University Football office and asked to speak with the athletic trainer, Jeff "Fergie" Ferguson. Fergie was Anthony's athletic trainer at the time of his death. On this call, he told me I should call Mutual of Omaha. Later that year, Fergie left Kansas State University and joined the NFL as a trainer for the San Francisco 49ers. It's disturbing that at no time after Anthony died did anyone at Kansas State University, the KSU Athletic Department, or the Kansas State University Football Front Office, tell me of the existence of such a "sudden death benefit" or life insurance policy. After years of visits to the university, conducting ABF Heart-Screening events, and supporting Anthony's alma mater, they didn't even have the courtesy or decency to inform me about this "sudden death benefit" policy!

After several phone calls and tear-filled discussions, I uncovered this horrifying life-insurance policy held by the NCAA on all college athletes. The accidental death policy would cover the usual type of transportation accidents and had the "cardiac clause" for Sudden Cardiac Deaths. The NCAA took out this policy in the unfortunate occurrence of an athlete's death during a college-sanctioned event. At the time of Anthony's death, the insurance company didn't consider that his death occurred during a university event (college-sanctioned event.) Anthony had been driving away from the KSU Football complex, but moments before his death, Anthony was in the KSU weight room. However, he left the football complex and drove two blocks when he had a Sudden Cardiac Arrest. I had to prove to the "insurance company" that he died during the "cool-down" phase of his heart after the KSU weight training. With a letter from the leading HCM researcher, Dr. Barry Maron, Mutual of Omaha agreed to payout Anthony's death benefit.

On July 31, 2000, the NCAA death benefit amount was $10,000. How could that be my son's life worth to the university, the NCAA, and the world? My research showed that a college-age young person's life is <u>worth over $2.5 million</u>. There is quite a disparity between $10,000 and $2.5 million! Besides, to add salt to my deep wound, the day after Anthony's death, the NCAA and Mutual of Omaha raised the death benefit amount to a meager $25,000, which was just $15,000 more. These young athletes' lives are grossly undervalued! The amount awarded to me was an embarrassing paltry sum of $10,000.

Why would the NCAA choose to carry life insurance on their athletes covering cardiac death and turn their backs on university student-athlete heart-screenings? I tried to understand this disconnect in logic. There may be disparities with resources to support mass screenings within the NCAA world. There may also be disparities in the health-care resources to support mass screenings. Additionally, in the U.S. there are not enough doctors, machines, or technicians to host heart-screening events simultaneously across the country for all 460,000 NCAA athletes and growing. Therefore, they roll the dice with an insurance policy to protect their assets if a student-athlete dies during a game or sanctioned event. The NCAA started carrying a "cardiac clause" in their life insurance "accidental death" policy in 1998. This is two years after the American Heart Association recommended "some kind of cardiac screening" be administered to young athletes. *Convenient or suspicious?*

The NCAA has affiliated colleges and universities nationwide, consisting of 460,000 young athletes. The NCAA student population is in stark contrast compared to the 8 million high school athletes. The "benefit payout risk" for the NCAA is small compared to high-school sports. I believe there are many questions the NCAA needs to answer. We need to educate parents about the risks of Sudden Cardiac Arrest, step up, and ask these crucial questions to hold the NCAA, medical professionals, and the giant pharmaceutical companies accountable. Remember, Duke University and the partnership with pharmaceutical giants (CSRC) was created to make cardiac drugs safer. The CSRC research and the business of the NCAA is not aligned to advance scientific knowledge on cardiac safety and prevention of Sudden Cardiac Arrest. Much of the multiple decades of research has warned of the dangers of SCA risks in children. In my humble opinion, the unscreened, young athletes were not important enough, because the profit made by keeping these young athletes playing outweighed the concern to protect their lives with low-cost heart-screenings.

In 2015, the research study from Tel Aviv, Isreal claimed it would cost them over $69 *billion* to screen all their athletes over twenty years. However, in those twenty years, they would only save 4,800 lives! Where is the NCAA or these researchers from another country getting their numbers?

The Anthony Bates Foundation tells a different story based on experience and facts. With the model built by the non-profit world of screening, ABF and our Trained Teams show that screening all the NCAA athletes, over twenty years, would cost substantially less, at $4 billion. The heart-screening results would have a finding of 2.5% with abnormal results. This translates to saving over 230,000 young lives from Possible Life-Threatening Sudden Cardiac Arrest in twenty years. That translates to saving approximately 11,500 young athletes each year.

Now, is that "important" enough for the NCAA?

How would anyone let a child or a young athlete die of a preventable cardiac malady? The NCAA has access to dozens of research studies done on cardiac incidence in children. Unfortunately, by the time these student-athletes are in college, they are adults. They sign their lives away, and these student-athletes are often taken advantage of by the profit motive. Parents and athletes need to take a stand to make a difference in their heart health. Every young life is vital to the future of our country. Every person deserves to live to full adulthood and enjoy his or her "golden years." Every family deserves "health and hope" over "death and grief."

CHAPTER THIRTY-SIX

Forgiveness!

21-Day Meditation – Hope in Uncertain Times

Forgiveness - Oprah Winfrey, Day 20

Oprah explains the forgiveness concepts so eloquently, "I've always loved an "ah-ha" moment. It's when you hear something that opens up a window in your mind and reminds you of your life and your view in life in a completely new way. I once had something even bigger than an "ah-ha" moment; I call it one of the most transcendent moments. It was when I fully understood the meaning of forgiveness defined in this way. A guest on Oprah's show said, *"Forgiveness is giving up the hope that the past could have been any different."* That resonated so deeply with me. "It" being able to let go and not being held hostage for another minute by the past. When you know and accept that it could not have been any different. Forgiveness doesn't mean you condone a behavior or make a wrong into a right. It simply means you give yourself permission to accept and release that what was done has been done. If you haven't been able to forgive, then you are holding onto something. You want it to be different. It takes a lot of energy to hold a grudge. The truth is, if you are holding a grudge, that grudge is also holding you. Here's a huge misperception: not forgiving someone doesn't give you power, it's actually poisoning you. Forgiveness is something you do for yourself. Not for the person who wronged you. And, by giving up the hope and accepting that what has happened has happened, you tap into the healing power of hope. You shift! You become a source of hope for other people, especially yourself and other people's own need to forgive and be forgiven. So, forgive yourself. Forgive others in the light of hope gets to gleam brighter."

Oprah's description of forgiveness resonated with me on many levels – a transcendent moment – on my path to forgiveness. As my partner, Will Maier, likes to say, "Forgiveness is the first step to enlightenment." It is a profound realization that when you know and accept that any event that occurs in your life could not have happened any other way than it did.

Through all the healing and growth I achieved from the Unity of Phoenix Chaplain Program, I found myself praying for my family and particularly my sister, Teresa! I had lost the relationship with her because we both were grieving in separate ways. We became disconnected as a family and as friends. She blamed me for my son's death by allowing Anthony to play football; she told me I was responsible for his death. As I said, we were both grieving, but the way we did it was not helpful to one another.

I could not change her opinion, as our relationship spiraled out of control, and I couldn't help her understand. I was blaming myself for the loss of our sisterhood. For my well-being, I had to step away from the pain of our fragmented relationship. However, through the encouragement of my partner, Will, Teresa and I finally reconnected a few years ago. Teresa's daughter, my niece, Angie, got married to a wonderful man, Alex. Although I remained guarded with appropriate boundaries, I stepped in to rekindle our relationship. She will always be my sister and Anthony's Auntie Teresa. She also suffered from the unhealed pain of her childhood. She, too, grieved the loss of my son, albeit differently from me. Anthony was her nephew, and she had loved him, too. Her grief came out initially as anger towards me. That, to her, was the only way she knew how to express it at the time.

My mother, Edna, grieved, too. Besides losing her daughters to the darkness, and anger, of their childhood hurt and abuse, she had now lost her grandson. We were swirling around in our sorrow, not realizing that each of us was also troubled and grieving in their way. We hurt so many loved ones without understanding the pain we struggled with was also the pain they struggled with as well. Finding healing from this pain is a gift of love. Without healing our soul, grief, and suffering, we will continue to hurt ourselves and other vital relationships in our lives.

I forgave my mother, Edna, for the loss of my childhood innocence. I felt all my family relationships were "dead to me" at some point in life, and I had to forgive myself for embracing that. I had to learn to let it go and release the pain I carried around in my heart. The pain no longer served me in the present and had to release it to make room for the love and life I wanted to have. I knew that holding on to the pain would eat me alive. I had to overcome that unresolved pain before the pain turns into cancer, sickness, or addiction that could not quickly be healed. I pray that you can forgive yourself and your family before it is too late; they will be there for you during a crisis and you for them. Isn't that what family is about? To find true forgiveness, we must heal our broken hearts.

The statistic in the U.S. for failed marriages after the death of a child is ninety percent.

Let that sink in, *Ninety percent.*

What about the statistic for failed friendships after the death of a child? Could it be similar, higher, or about the same? I have looked intently at my relationships and friendships throughout my life. Only about ten percent of the friends I have now are the same ones I had before Anthony died. For me, the statistic is about the same, ninety percent of those friendships no longer exist. The one common thread was the loss of my child. That will create distance and uncomfortable feelings for people who can't relate to that kind of loss. People don't know what to say, how to react, or what to do. Sadly, many of those friendships have fallen away.

My youngest sister, Diane, was spared most of the abuses of our childhood. She probably had experienced other issues through the verbal abuses and put-downs by screaming parents, particularly my stepfather. She had her own adult "drama and trauma" to heal from her broken marriage and an abusive husband. However, I don't believe those two pedophiles, my stepfather, Jim, and my stepbrother, Jimmy, ever abused my youngest sister.

Anthony was able to see his Auntie Diane the most frequently during the early years of his life, as she lived with us when he was about two years old. There were times that Diane was mistaken for Anthony's mother, as they had similar features. We shared an apartment, and she eventually got her place. Diane even worked for my then future-husband, Allen, at Safelite Auto Glass. We did a lot together as a family.

When Diane had her family, sons Troy and Chase, we noticed similarities in Chase and Anthony's features. They had large builds and loved sports. Chase and Anthony were not only cousins but "brothers from another mother!" Diane and her boys came to Anthony's funeral. They cried and grieved his loss as well.

In 2006, several years after Anthony died, Diane's oldest son, Troy, a Marine at the time, had orders to ship off to Afghanistan. Ironically, Troy, stationed at Camp Pendleton between San Diego and Los Angeles, was close to Disneyland. With his growing family, wife Jennifer, and young son, Tristan, they could join us in Disneyland for a family send-off. My older sister, Brenda, brought her daughters, Lanie and Gabrielle, from Montana, and Diane and Chase flew in from Alabama. I surprised our mother with the trip to Disneyland. We all drove over from Phoenix to Los Angeles to meet up with Troy and his family. We surprised Troy by bringing his brother, Chase. It was a wonderful time and a profound healing event for all of us. It was great to be back together with my sisters and mother. Remember, forgiveness is the first step to enlightenment!

Family is essential in the healing of grief. We have to stick together. The new times we enjoyed allowed us to heal and make new, happy memories. Time together will help heal the souls that hide from their sorrow. Put family first. Loneliness is your alternative. I experienced loneliness for many years after Anthony died. We are each on a journey of healing, some slower, some faster than others. Be gentle with yourself, and be gentle with your family.

Each of us is on an individual path in the healing process. After that fun-filled trip to Disneyland, Troy didn't deploy to Afghanistan for circumstances he did not reveal to me. Years later, I stopped communicating with hm because of his inappropriate behaviors in life. I am sad about that.

Another lesson I learned from the Unity of Phoenix Chaplain Program was to "set boundaries." I had to set boundaries to prevent the destructive and abusive behaviors in some of my family members' lives from upsetting my life. I needed my soul healing, and I couldn't rescue anyone other than myself, then or now. For Troy and others in my family, I had to keep my distance for my true healing. I had to enact my own effective "damage control" regarding Troy and other family members, the same way I dealt with "damage control" after Anthony's death. I pray for Troy, his family, his journey to forgiveness, truth, love, and peace. Life is a large schoolroom where lessons unfold for us to learn. If we don't learn them, the universe has beautiful ways of bring back these lessons to us, in different forms, until we "get it."

"Not my circus, not my monkeys." The realization that other people's problems are not mine to mess in is an additional lesson I learned as a Unity of Phoenix Chaplain. I am not here to solve other people's problems, only support their healing journey through prayer and love. We must set our healthy boundaries, allow people to heal, and love them while we support our safety, health, and life.

CHAPTER THIRTY-SEVEN

Conclusion

Even with creating a non-profit and supporting many new organizations, there were numerous hurdles to overcome. The economic challenges, the lack of NCAA support, and the continued struggle to find new and repeat financial donors weigh heavily on our small ABF non-profit organizations' sustainability. When the economy is good, the donations are plentiful, and ABF can offer screenings and community resources to improve Sudden Cardiac Arrest (SCA) outcomes. The recent change in the tax laws has decreased the amount a person can deduct for charitable donations, which has adversely affected many small charities like ABF. Expendable income is also a challenge for lower-income families when it comes to paying fees for heart-screenings. In times like today, we have both the health and economic fears brought on by this current COVID-19 pandemic, while the average American struggles to make ends meet with less than $400 in the bank. Donating to any charity is not on the mind of the average American.

Both poor and rich people are losing children to Sudden Cardiac Death. Those with compassion and "heart" are the ones who are saving the children. Parent Heart Watch (PHW) families and the programs are springing up because of the increased need to improve young athletes' heart-health in making sports safer for children. That is, it should always be the goal.

Research takes time. I see that in all the programs created in the name of heart health. <u>Prevention of Sudden Cardiac Death</u> continues to be ignored by large institutions such as the American Heart Association (AHA) and significant sporting leagues such as the NCAA. Parents everywhere need to be educated about possible heart health problems in their children, and risks from Sudden Cardiac Arrest before a child dies. Parents will move the needle. Parents need to get directly involved, get their children screened, and raise their collective voices to reach the NCAA and High School Sports Authorities. These organizations must listen and make the appropriate, long-overdue changes to save more of our young athletes' lives. This initiative move started by a grassroots parental, medical, and philosophical movement, of epic proportions, begs the big question: ***"What's more important lives or box scores?"*** Big businesses, the NCAA and its universities have to wake up and change the way they value their student-athletes' lives. These requests should be non-negotiable!

Change takes money, too. Money is the energy toward creating the change. Jane Goodall didn't come back from Africa and throw her hands in the air, complaining, "I'm only one person" and couldn't help the creatures in need. She advocated for the chimps; she did the fundraising to help her cause and to move the needle towards hope for those creatures.

The NCAA and the other wealthy corporations make millions by exploiting young athletes who put their lives on the line, in potentially dangerous activities. Yet, young athletes do not receive a dime of compensation. We must hold these corporations accountable for the deaths of these athletes who were not adequately heart-screened. We need support for a nationwide heart-screening program within the universities and sports teams. Lives are on the line, if not today, tomorrow. Empowered athletes and their parents should take a stand for the health-safety of their children. Sudden Cardiac Death is not predictable, but it is preventable.

Sudden Cardiac Arrest survivors and stories of new saves now fill the Heart-2-Heart Parent Heart Watch Conference each year. Passion, Prevention, Protection, and Perseverance are the keys to building the foundation for the next generation to continue the mission of protecting young athletes. The experiences of the young people saved from SCA these past twenty years have filled my heart full of amazement and encouragement. All the sacrifices made by the parents who lost their child too soon, have made a difference in many other families' lives. However, I am still heartsick by the stories, in the news media and on social media, of the children that continue to die from preventable sudden cardiac death.

There are numerous industry breakthroughs in the fifteen years since the inception of Parent Heart Watch founded by four grieving mothers. In the January 2020 Heart-2-Heart Parent Heart Watch Conference, their presentations were emblazoned with announcements of continual improvement in saving young lives.

Announced at the 2020 PHW meeting, another group of young people created Archer First Response System to fly a drone with an Automatic External Defibrillator (AED) and a first responder first-aid kit to an emergency scene, within seven square miles, in less than five minutes. They are already creating phase two of their product to fly thirty square miles in less than five minutes. The products could launch in late 2020. The advancements of the Archer First Response System is an exciting technology breakthrough done by the youth of this nation.

Research groups within the Parent Heart Watch family have sprung out of work needed. In 2000, Karen and John Acompora created the Louis Acompora Foundation after the death of their son, Louis, during a lacrosse game. Louis died due to Commotio Cordis, in his case, a ball strike to his chest that caused his healthy heart to quiver, and only the shock from an AED may have saved him. Initially, the Louis Acompora Foundation concentrated their efforts on AED placement. Soon after, they learned the lacrosse industry needed better chest protectors. The Louis Acompora Foundation partnered with the lacrosse industry to fund needed research to build better chest protectors in that sport. By 2021, new chest protectors will be mandatory for men's lacrosse. The women's lacrosse will take a year or so longer, but it's coming.

Our ABF Trained Teams with a young heart-screening organization are now taking center stage. One California group of students, Saving

Hearts Foundation, created heart-screening at their college, University of California Los Angeles (UCLA.) They built a local chapter program to share with Greek societies at other universities. These students are in year three and rolling the expansion efforts out across the country. Saving Hearts Foundation will train others to help prepare even more people to "screen young hearts and save young lives!"

Another young group of students from the Massachusetts Institute of Technology (MIT) created Avive, to become an AED manufacturer, that would outfit an AED into new cars and homes, businesses, and our personal lives. This group founded by our friend, Sameer Jafri and his MIT pals, is an offshoot of the UCLA ABF Trained Team, Saving Hearts Foundation. We are excited about their breakthroughs, ingenuity, continued collaborations, and perseverance to launch new life-saving products.

In December 2007, Rafe Maccarone died in the arms of his friends during soccer practice. Like my Anthony, Rafe died from undiagnosed HCM. His mother and father, Valerie and Ralph, with Rafe's teenage friends, Evan Ernst, Cam Vermette, and Katie Hardcastle, created Who We Play For (WWPF.) They became another ABF Trained Team screening group in Florida. Recently, WWPF started screening in their school districts, and now all the student-athletes will be tested and given an electrocardiogram (ECG/EKG) from WWPF. They are marching across the state of Florida. WWPF has introduced its program in additional states as well.

Parent groups are affecting the nation, too! The Parent Heart Watch family out of Texas is the Cody Stephens Foundation – "Go Big or Go Home." Scott and Melody Stephens created this movement after their son Cody died on May 26, 2012, from undiagnosed HCM. The Cody Stephens Foundation approached the state legislature to provide a better screening program in Texas high school sports. In 2019, the Texas group "Go Big or Go Home" helped pass a vital law requiring an "opt-in" for parents to be informed of cardiac issues and offered an ECG/EKG through their screening program. Pennsylvania just passed a similar bill into law with the Payton Walker Foundation and California is looking to pass similar laws. These were all spearheaded by Parent Heart Watch families!

With fundraising and legislative efforts, the Cody Stephens Foundation initially collaborated with Cypress Cardiac Project to administer Electrocardiogram (ECG/EKG) screenings across the Southwest. Over time, Cypress Cardiac Project merged with the Cody Stephens Foundation. Cardiologist, Dr. Thomas deBauche, has performed ECG/EKG screenings on young athletes for decades in Texas. He has been one of the trailblazers and "Heart Champions" to advocate for youth for longer than ABF has been providing screenings. Thank you, Dr. deBauche!

Parent Heart Watch (PHW) families are working on Sudden Cardiac Arrest advancements in many corners of this country. My own heart-felt blessing comes through seeing the continuing stages of our work, developing programs that protect children's hearts. The 2030 goal of PHW is to eliminate preventable Sudden Cardiac Arrest in children. Join in this promise and take a stand for children and families everywhere.

I know my son will never come back to me in this physical world. I have accepted this reality – I have accepted that the outcome could not have been any different. However, I also know in my heart that we will meet again in Heaven. When I was a new member at that little little Kansas community church, I spoke with our pastor one night prayer circle. I told him of my vision that night, during the prayer circle: "I saw myself above the clouds, looking down on the world. I got the distinct impression that my life was going to be important to the world!" I didn't know that my son would die in ten years, and my whole life would be about helping the world. I took a stand for children, and with one step at a time over these past years, I have overcome the hurt, brokenness, struggles, and many tragedies to still stand for what I believe; health, peace, and love!

For years after Anthony's death, I was angry. I was mad at him that he left me through his death. When I grieved my son, I was also still upset with other men who had abused, neglected, or disappointed me. I was still angry with my mother for not believing me about the abuse I had received. I became angry with my younger sister, Teresa, for blaming me for Anthony's death. I have finally found out that I am, once "damaged," now whole and making my life meaningful. I HAVE FORGIVEN THEM ALL -- AS WELL AS MYSELF.

I have also learned to forgive Kansas State University and the NCAA! I don't condone the behavior of institutions that put their student athletes health at a low priority. Profits over health do not make sense to me.

I just needed to follow my heart, and my life would unfold perfectly in front of me.

A New Decade for the Anthony Bates Foundation

In 2019, our volunteer-intern, Martie Combs, DNP, MSN-Ed, RN, worked on her Doctor of Nurse Practice (DNP) project with the ABF data to improve our Electrocardiogram (ECG/EKG) tests. She discovered a rate of artifact in our ECGs at thirty percent. We describe ECG artifact as electrical noise from elsewhere in the body (muscle tension or talking), poor ECG electrode contact, and possible machine malfunction. The key to ECG screening tests' quality is proper ECG electrode placement and capturing a good tracing of the heart rhythm. In her DNP project, Dr. Combs created an online course that required our ABF volunteers to take when they work the ECG stations at our ABF Heart-Screening events. Through the ABF ECG Certification Training Course, ABF volunteers improved their electrode placement and reduced the artifact on the ECG tracings to five-percent, a twenty-five percent improvement! Our quality improvement course is available to our ABF Trained Teams. With this course upgrade, we hope to remove the "roadblock" in the medical community related to "false positives" in screenings.

Just before the COVID-19 pandemic lockdown, I traveled to Boston, Massachusetts, to present at the annual National Collegiate Emergency Medical Services Foundation (NCEMSF) conference. While in Boston, in late February 2020, ABF presented the ABF ECG Certification Training Course to future EMS first responders. More than forty students attended the presentation. Several students enthusiastically announced during and after the event that they would be working on setting up heart-screenings on their campuses. Post-pandemic, students will want to find ways to support life through early detection of heart issues. There is hope for more heart-screening programs for the youth of our nation. We need to help these young people save the children in their communities.

By 2019, ABF had screened over 15,600 young hearts, finding thirteen-percent with problems and a consistent two-percent with "Possible Life-Threatening" issues. There are more than seventy-five active ABF Trained Teams in the U.S. Each team is hosting community heart-screenings; 2020 figures showed the young hearts screened by our ABF Trained Teams to be more than 1,013,745. Our ABF Trained Teams are training other teams. Including these numbers, in our count, we have surpassed 1 million screened before 2020 – even surrounded by this COVID-19 pandemic.

The impact of life's unexpected events is truly immeasurable. My life is full of many examples of how actions of love and forgiveness can heal the suffering of shared grief. Twenty years ago, I began a one-person quest by starting a new, tiny organization to begin "screening young hearts and saving young lives!" I did this so that parents would not have to suffer my loss. Now we have grown and evolved into a whole country of Anthony Bates Foundation Trained Teams of "screeners" that have amassed saving over 20,000 lives. Our ABF Trained Teams are continuing to train and empower others.

Amid the COVID-19 pandemic, schools have been shuttered, and sporting events canceled all over the world. I know in my heart, this too shall pass. Due to circumstances out of my control, it may take some time to get back to "screening young hearts and saving young lives!" in the schools. In the meantime, I decided to go back to school to obtain a certificate in cardiac ultrasound. I then plan to start writing the next chapters in my life and for ABF. We will continue to help communities and children everywhere. Thank you for letting me share my life and my mission with you. I hope you enjoyed my heart. Be well. Stay safe. Be at peace!

We have reached our 2020 goal:

TO SCREEN OVER ONE MILLION HEARTS!

If you believe in our ABF mission:

If you believe that more children should and can be saved through proper heart-screenings, join us.

WILL YOU JOIN US TO MAKE A DIFFERENCE IN COMMUNITIES EVERYWHERE? TOGETHER LET'S "SCREEN MORE HEARTS AND SAVE MORE LIVES!"

For more information and to join the cause, go to www.AnthonyBates.org

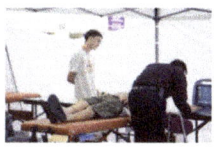

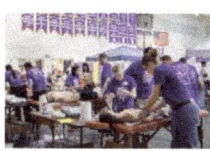

References

Lightning Source UK Ltd.
Milton Keynes UK
UKHW020432011220
374381UK00005B/375/J

9 781641 844369